CW01239103

Leicestershire Events

The Market Place in Loughborough, showing the preparations involved for marking Edward VII's coronation in 1902.

Leicestershire Events

Malcolm Elliott

Phillimore

2004

Published by
PHILLIMORE & CO. LTD
Shopwyke Manor Barn, Chichester, West Sussex, England

© Malcolm Elliott, 2004

ISBN 1 86077 280 3

Printed and bound in Great Britain by
CAMBRIDGE PRINTING

Contents

List of Illustrations VI
Acknowledgements X
Introduction XII

1. The Early History of Leicestershire 1
2. After Bosworth 8
3. Nobility and Notoriety 16
4. Fox Hunting 26
5. Leicestershire at Leisure 35
6. In Time of War 49
7. Crime and Punishment 57
8. Transportation 67
9. Acts of God 89
10. Civic and Royal Events 102
11. Social Events 121

Select Bibliography 129
Index 130

List of Illustrations

Frontispiece: The Market Place in Loughborough, 1902

1. Statue in Watermead Park 1
2. Dr Patrick Clay holding a bronze handle from an Iron-Age tankard 2
3. The Jewry Wall as illustrated in Nichols' *History of Leicestershire* (1791) 3
4. Cardinal Wolsey entering Leicester Abbey. 6
5. The Church at Lutterworth 7
6. The Gatehouse of Kirby Muxloe Castle 9
7. Bradgate House as it is today 10
8. Portrait of Lady Jane Grey 10
9. Ulverscroft Priory, sketched by Mrs F.F. Palmer. 11
10. Great Stretton Church as it is today 12
11. The Church and Hall at Goadby Marwood north of Melton Mowbray. 13
12. The church and hall at Staunton Harold. 14
13. The stockinger 15
14. Ashby Castle today 17
15. Breaches in the Town Walls made by royalist troops during the Civil War 18
16. The Siege of Leicester, 1645, as illustrated in John Nichols 19
17. Braunstone Hall from the illustration in John Nichols 21
18. Plaque in Bradgate Park. 23
19. John Henry, 5th Duke of Rutland 24
20. Statue in Leicester Market Place 25
21. Coleorton Hall built in 1805 for Sir George Beaumont 25
22. Her Majesty Queen Elizabeth is seen here at a pie factory in Melton, 1996. 26
23. Workers in the yard of Tebbutt's Pork Pie factory, about 1895 27
24. Advertisement for pork pies. 28
25. The First Stilton Cheese Fair in Sherard Street, Melton Mowbray in 1883 28
26. A fox hunter enjoying a Melton pork pie 29
27. 'Painting the Town Red' 30
28. The Midnight Hunt 31
29. The Cottesmore Hunt ignored the pleas of a crossing keeper 31
30. Hoby water-mill, 1874, several gentlemen attempting to cross a plank bridge 32
31. The Fernie hounds gathering at Wistow, 1927 32
32. The Prince of Wales and Mrs Simpson at Craven Lodge, 1935. 33
33. The Prince of Wales, the future Edward VIII, riding to hounds 34
34. The last fair in Humberstone Gate, 1904 36
35. Bottle-kicking in 1993 38
36. Bottle-kicking in 1993 39
37. Bottle-kicking in 2003 39

38. Sporting Triumph, the statue commemorating Leicester's sporting success 43
39. The old hall at Kirkby Mallory before it was demolished 44
40. Programme for *HMS Pinafore* with all three Attenborough boys in the cast list 45
41. The Princess and Sir Richard Attenborough at the Opening of the Centre 45
42. Elephants being taken to Bertram Mills' Circus at Melton Mowbray, 1935 46
43. The May Fair at Castle Donington 46
44. Mafeking celebrations in Market Harborough 49
45. 5th Territorial Battalion of the Leicestershire Regiment, 1914 50
46. Signing-up for service in the Great War at the Magazine in Leicester 50
47. Peace celebrations, Shepshed, 1919 51
48. Children being entertained at the Picture House, Loughborough, 1914 52
49. Damage caused by a Zeppelin raid on Loughborough in 1916 53
50-1. Children collecting aluminium and boys filling sand bags 54-5
52. Evacuees coming to Loughborough to escape from the Blitz 56
53. Remembrance Day at Castle Hill, 1992 56
54. The interior of Bottesford church with the Manners monuments 58
55. Gibbet in the Guildhall 52
56. A newspaper illustration of the last days of James Cook, 1832 63
57. 'Tanky' Smith in one of his disguises 63
58. Ronald Light, accused of murder 64
59. The scene of the crime, on the Gartree road, near Little Stretton 64
60. The bicycle hauled from the canal 65
61. Sir Alex Jeffries receiving the Freedom of the City 66
62. The Tollgate on Thorpe Road, Loughborough 68
63. The last stage coach leaving the *Three Crowns Inn* in 1866 68
64. Copy of a bill for bed and breakfast at the *Three Crowns* in 1841 69
65-6. The Blackbrook Reservoir under construction, completed in 1906 70-1
67. A regatta on the canal at Market Harborough in 1909 74
68. The Swannington inclined plane 75
69. The building of the Midland Railway 76
70. Thomas Cook's Temperance Hall and Hotel in Granby Street 76
71-2. Two of the panels on the offices of Thomas Cook 77
73. The Great Central at Stanford 77
74. A giant bell made for St Paul's Cathedral in London by Taylor's bell foundry ... 78
75. The Bell, known as Great Paul, being transported to London 78
76. The Bell cast by Taylors of Loughborough arriving at St Paul's Cathedral 79
77. Foxton Locks with the Lift on the Horizon 79
78. Tramlines being laid at the junction of London Road and Evington Road 80
79. The last horse-drawn tram at the Clock Tower in 1904 80
80. A Hansom cab also passes the Clock Tower in the same year 80
81. A motor car at Cossington in 1897 81
82. The construction of the M1 as it passed through South Leicestershire 82
83. An accident on the M1 motorway near the junction with the M6, 2003 83
84. Advertisement for a 'Coronation' balloon ascent in 1824 84
85. Pilcher's original 'Hawk' glider 84
86. Gustav Hamel bringing the first-ever delivery of newspapers by air 85
87. A 70hp Bleriot at Loughborough, at the 1912 *Daily Mail* Aero Circuit 85
88. Taylorcraft Auster Mark 3 86
89. Auster Air Display at Rearsby 87
90. A plane attempting an emergency landing at East Midlands airport 88

91.	Collapse of the Geography Building at Leicester University in 1983	89
92.	South Croxton Church struck by lightning 1936	90
93.	Sketch of snow drifts on the road to Market Harborough	91
94.	Impression of the Crow Mills flood at South Wigston, 1852	91
95.	Market Harborough, awash with water in December 1900	92
96.	Floods in Melton Mowbray in 1900	92
97.	Market Street, Ashby de la Zouch flooded to four feet	93
98.	Floodwater at the Brush works in Loughborough in December 1910	94
99.	Floods at the junction of Ashby Road and Derby Road, Loughborough	95
100.	A flooded road at Dishley in August 1912	95
101.	A charabanc driving through water on Derby Road	96
102.	A view of the drying-up of reservoir at Swithland, 1929	97
103.	Elmesthorpe, 1914, a fire destroyed one of the Countess Lovelace's cottages	98
104-5.	Scenes at the pit head	99
106.	The memorial tablet in Whitwick church	100
107.	A young worker in the brick-yards	101
108.	Ashby de la Zouch celebrates Queen Victoria's Golden Jubilee in 1887	102
109.	Jubilant crowds, bandsmen and rifle volunteers celebrate in Ashby de la Zouch	103
110.	Jubilee celebrations at Ashby de la Zouch, 1887	104
111.	The Market Place, Loughborough, 1887	105
112.	Planting a tree in Leicester's Victoria Park, 1897	106
113.	The Market Place in Loughborough, showing Edward VII's coronation in 1902	107
114.	A huge bonfire, 40 feet high, was lit in honour of Edward's accession	108
115.	Festivities marking the Coronation of George V, Ashby de la Zouch	108
116.	A civic procession passing along Granby Street in Loughborough, 1911	109
117.	Presentation of commemorative mugs for the coronation of George V	110
118.	The coronation celebrated in Loughborough, 1911	111
119.	The inhabitants of Kibworth enjoy May Day in 1908	112
120.	Cemetery Chapels in Welford Road Cemetery	113
121.	Mary Linwood	113
122.	An Exhibition of Fine Art held in New Walk, January 1885	113
123.	The Hustings at the election of 1826	114
124.	Close of Poll in the Market Place, 1826	114
125.	The Prince and Princess of Wales open Abbey Park, 29 May 1882	115
126.	Princess Alexandra planting an oak tree in Abbey Park	115
127.	Lutyens' War Memorial in Victoria Park, Leicester	117
128.	The Carillon at Loughborough during the opening ceremony in 1934	117
129.	Laying the foundation stone of the Clock Tower, 1868	118
130.	The Opening Ceremony for Loughborough Endowed School, 1850	119
131.	Loughborough Grammar School	120
132.	Celebratory dinner in the bell mouth of the new sewer, 1895	120
133.	March of Unemployed Men to London, 1905	123
134.	The men stopping overnight at Market Harborough	123
135.	Monks building at St Bernard's Abbey in Charnwood Forest in the 1930s	124
136.	The Baptist Chapel on Belvoir Street, from the *Illustrated London News*, 1845	125
137.	The advertisement which was placed in the *Uganda Argus* in 1972	126
138.	A young girl holding a diva lamp during Diwali, 2003	127
139.	Mosque in Evington Road	127
140.	Dancers at the Caribbean Carnival on Victoria Park, 2001	128

Acknowledgements

A book of this nature must depend on numerous original sources, be they books, pamphlets, articles or casual conversations. I have tried to record all my debts, but there must remain facts, gathered over time, the source of which it is no longer possible to identify. For these I can only offer a gereral 'thank you' to all who have helped me to an appreciation of Leicestershire history and the events selected here.

For the pictures used I wish to thank the staff of the Leicestershire Record Office at South Wigston for their unfailing courtesy and for permission to use illustrations number 3, 4, 9, 10, 12, 15-17, 21, 31, 33-4, 39, 45-6, 56, 58-60, 62-3, 68-9, 70, 77-82, 84 92, 102-3, 112, 117, 123-4, 129, 133-4. I am indebted also to the staff of the library at Market Harborough for providing me with illustrations 44, 67 and 95 and for 35 and 36 which were taken by the late Mick Cheney and to his widow, Mrs Cheney, for allowing me to use the splendid action shots of Hallaton bottle-kicking in 1993. My thanks are also due to Andrew Carpenter for the photograph, number 37, he provided of the same event in 2003. The staff at Loughborough Library were wonderfully accommodating and allowed me to copy from their collection numbers 42-3, 47-53, 64-6, 73, 86-7, 97-9, 111, 113-4, 116, 118 and 128. For all these I must also thank the County Archivist, Dr Carl Harrison, and Mrs Margaret Bellamy, the Head of Library Services, for kindly allowing me to make use of the material under their control.

My other great debt is to the Library of the University of Leicester and to their chief photographer, Colin Brooks, for enabling me to use illustrations from their collection, numbers 2, 5, 8, 19, 61, 74-6, 91, 94, 107, 109, 120-2, 125-6, 130-1, 135-6. I wish to thank also Mrs Barbara Browse for enabling me to use illustration 13, of a stockinger, in her copy of *Leicestershire* by Pingriff, published in 1920. I owe a great debt to Trevor Hickman who generously allowed me to use illustrations 27-30 and 32 from his *Melton Mowbray Album*. My thanks also to Kenneth Hillier and the Ashby Heritage Group for permission to use numbers 93, 110 and 115, from the book *Around Ashby-de-la-Zouch*.

I wish to thank my friend Joan Watson for the use of her programme for *H.M.S. Pinafore*, 40. The Richard Attenborough Centre for Disability and the Arts kindly provided illustration 41, taken by Doug McKenzie of Beckenham, Kent. Jim Tomlinson of *The Hinckley Times* was most helpful in searching the paper's library of photographs, and illustration 83 was taken from there. The original Percy Pilcher flying machine is to be found in the National Museums of Scotland's Museum of Flight in East Lothian, whence illustration 85 was selected. The shot of the M I crash near Kegworth came from *The Times*, and those of Auster Aircraft were kindly provided by Mr Mike Preston of the Auster Aero Club Heritage Group.

Whitwick Historical Group gave me permission to use the illustrations from their book, *Banded Together*, on the Whitwick Mine Disaster, numbers 104-106. Stuart Warburton, Principal Managing Curator of the Leicester City Museums, kindly provided the slide of a celebratory dinner in the sewer from which number 132 was taken. 138 and 140 were provided by Dave Harris of Creativity Works, for whose assistance I am more than grateful. The remaining photographs are my own.

In addition to the photographic material, I am indebted to the following for their help in allowing me to use material from their published works on Leicestershire: to Mr Roy Bailey for quotations from his *Portrait of Leicestershire* published in 1977; to Brian Williams for permission to use his work on *An Exploration of the Lost Charnwood Forest Canal*; to Phillip Scaysbrook for his book on *The Civil War in Leicestershire and Rutland*; to John Morrison for permission to use his splendid study of *Hallaton, Hare Pie Scrambling and Bottle-Kicking*; and to the authors of articles in the *Transactions of the Leicestershire Archaeological and Historical Society*, Dr Davd Wykes on *The Riots of 1773 and 1789* and Jeremy Crump on *The Leicester Races*. My thanks also to Mr Roy Bonser for use of information about Sir Frank Whittle contained in his book *An Outline History of Aviation*.

For reading through my script and saving me from the embarrassment of factual, grammatical and stylistic errors I want to thank Richard Gill and John Bennett, who between them have an immense fund of knowledge on the county and an instinctive grasp of how to write. And finally, for putting up with all the disruption and stress that inevitably go with compiling a book such as this, and for rescuing me when the computer refuses to obey the simplest commands, I am, as always, most indebted to my wife.

INTRODUCTION

Just what do we mean by events? From the standpoint of the village pump every garden party and amateur theatrical is an event, but not many of these are remembered beyond the circle of dedicated souls intimately connected with the outcome. At the other extreme, some moments in time are immediately recognised as memorable and the stuff of history. Take the Kegworth air crash of 1989. It flashed instantly round the air waves of the world. Not only the human tragedy but the lessons learned for subsequent flights made it an event of national, if not world, significance.

If we stand back from our local vantage point and look at times in history when attention was fixed on happenings here in Leicestershire, we could single out several landmarks. The battle of Bosworth in 1485 is probably the most notable, but how can it be visualised in a pictorial history? Attempts at graphic representation, such as Victorian depictions of the death of Jane Grey, have no more validity than Hollywood melodramas.

Prehistory has left little trace of the incidents that shaped human destiny. Yet there must have been countless events in this central portion of the British Isles that uplifted or crushed the spirit of its earliest inhabitants. Even before man came to these parts, the eruption of the Charnian volcano, about 600 million years ago, was an event of surpassing magnitude that literally shaped the land on which human beings have lived ever since.

Between the advent of the first settlers and our first recorded history, tremors and landslides, fire and flood, must have brought as much anguish as in the relatively brief period we know as our 'history'. There would also have been times of jubilation at abundant harvests, but we have no evidence for these happenings and so, for the most part, the events in Leicestershire dealt with in this book concern the recent past, when photography captured the living moment and preserved the transient for posterity. I have attempted to flesh out the bare bones of earlier periods by recording events on which attention focused at the time or which subsequent generations have regarded as defining moments, to which we return as familiar milestones in our history. They may not in fact be important in themselves, but they give us our bearings and make it easier to think we understand the past and appreciate its relevance to our future.

One
THE EARLY HISTORY OF LEICESTERSHIRE

One of our earliest sagas is that set down by Geoffrey of Monmouth, a Benedictine monk, in the 12th century, concerning an ancient British monarch by the name of Lear.

Experts tell us that Leire was an old name for the river Soar, and it was probably here in Leicestershire that Shakespeare's immortal tale of senile stupidity and fillial impatience unfolded. According to Geoffrey of Monmouth, King Lear governed his country for sixty years and 'built upon the river Sore a city, called in the British tongue Kaerleir, in the Saxon, Leircestre'. Monmouth goes on to recount that Cordelia buried her father 'in a certain vault which she ordered to be made for him under the river Sore in Leicester'. Alas, the ancient texts upon which he claimed to base his story have never been found, and most scholars dismiss the whole story as without foundation, but there is a modern statue of Lear, mourning over the body of his dead daughter, in the stretch of water known as King Lear's Lake, just north of Leicester.

1 *Statue in Watermead Park: In the shallow waters of King Lear's Lake in Watermead Park, just north of Leicester, stands this modern sculpture, by David Hunter and others, of the King mourning over the body of the dead Cordelia. An information board tells us that Lear reigned in the eighth century B.C. and that he is supposed to have been buried in a vault 'downstream from Leicester' and possibly not far from the site of the sculpture.*

2 *Dr Patrick Clay, of Leicester University Archaeological Services, holds a bronze handle from an Iron-Age tankard. This is part of a hoard discovered in south-east Leicestershire in April 2003 by Ken Wallace, a retired university lecturer. Over three thousand gold and silver tokens were discovered.*

What we know of ancient British culture in these parts has been enormously enhanced by the finding of buried treasure in south-east Leicestershire. The work of Peter Liddle, Keeper of Archaeology for the Leicestershire Museums Service, and his team of enthusiastic field walkers carefully recording their finds of pottery and chiselled stones, was given national prominence in 2003, after the discovery of over 3,000 gold and silver coins and other material.

The site was most probably a holy place at which ritual offerings were made to the gods. Remains of animals found nearby, testify to the slaughter of sheep and dogs in sacrificial rites. The gold and silver coins or tokens are unlikely to have been used in commercial transactions as this was not a money economy and they bear no denominational marks or indication of their worth. It would seem that ritual offerings were made here to local deities.

Bearing in mind that this is a pre-Roman site, the discovery of a gilded Roman helmet was particularly exciting. It is thought that the local Celtic tribe, the Corieltauvi, were sympathetic to the Romans and that this may have been a gift to mark Roman appreciation for their collaboration.

The name Corieltauvi has been translated as 'the people of the land of many rivers'. The hoard apparently dates from the year before the Claudian invasion of A.D. 43, and the find has re-enforced the view that Leicestershire was a populous and thriving part of Celtic civilisation rather than just a rural backwater of a predominantly southern economy.

When Rome finally decided to subdue Celtic Britain, the legions trudged along the Fosse Way and probably forded the Soar somewhere near Leicester's West Bridge. It was a convenient stopping place on their march to the north, and an abundance of coinage and tessellated pavements testify to the ability of Romans to do as Rome did even in such a cold outpost of empire.

Leicester can claim the largest piece of Roman masonry in Britain in the edifice, known as the Jewry Wall, and at least twenty-six mosaic pavements have been unearthed in the town, indicating a level of sophistication and luxury not replicated till modern times. The Romans called the town Ratae Corieltauvi, the camp of the British people who inhabited the area at the time.

Ratae was a busy town with a huge central square or forum and basilica and a market area or macella that adjoined it to the north-west. Houses with under-floor heating and beautifully decorated walls and mosaic floors have been unearthed in and around Ratae. Fragments of pottery and the contents of waste pits tell of a civilisation that brought luxury and gracious living to its more fortunate citizens. The rest of humanity would not have enjoyed these luxuries and would no doubt have regarded the events pertaining to their Roman masters as having little to do with their own struggle for existence.

Legions garrisoned in Britain must have felt isolated and remote from the centre of action. It would have taken weeks for news to arrive from Rome and for fresh decrees to permeate such a far corner of its empire. When the final orders came to abandon the island, Ratae probably became something of a ghost town, left to decay, for its economic base had little in common with the way of life of the Anglo-Saxon peoples who lived here after the Romans withdrew.

The centuries following the departure of the legions are still commonly known as 'the Dark Ages'—'dark' because we know so little about them

3 *The Jewry Wall as illustrated in Nichols'* History of Leicestershire *(1791).*

compared with the written histories of Rome and of the Normans. Life in Saxon and Danish Leicestershire centred not in the towns, but in the country. Newcomers had to wrest areas of land from the wild if they could not take over earlier settlements. From the fifth century onwards they made their way up the river valleys and spread into the surrounding countryside, establishing as they did so a way of life that was essentially communal.

Each man had a portion of land on which to sow corn, taking his turn with the village plough, a heavy, wheel-less implement, dragged through the soil by the village ox-team. The plough share or mold-board turned the soil toward the centre of each strip or furlong, the furrow-long, creating the familiar pattern of ridge and furrow in the landscape. Each year, the crops would be grown on the next of two, or usually three, great open fields, thus ensuring a rotation that allowed the soil to lie fallow once in every three years. It was a pattern of agriculture that survived, in essence, till the lands were enclosed by wealthy individuals as their own, and very private, property.

Little is known of Anglo-Saxon social and political history, but there is no reason to suppose it was any less eventful or dramatic to men and women at the time than any other period of human existence. We read, for instance, of the treacherous murder of St Wistan, the young Saxon king who met his death at Wistow on 1 June 849. He was a saintly descendant of King Offa and he apparently persuaded his mother against marriage to one Beortfrith. Incensed at such interference in his matrimonial affairs, Beortfrith invited Wistan to a meeting and, while giving him the kiss of peace, landed a blow on his head with the hilt of his sword, his servants also piercing the saint's body. It is perhaps some comfort to know that Beortfrith at once became insane and Wistan's body was taken to Repton for burial.

Four decades later, the Danes subjugated the kingdom of Mercia, and Leicester became one of the five boroughs of the Danelaw, cut off from Anglo-Saxon Wessex by the ancient line of Watling Street which still forms the county's southern boundary. Early in the tenth century, Aethelfloeda, the daughter of Alfred the Great, succeeded in re-gaining control for the English without shedding a drop of blood. But tension between the inhabitants of Wessex and their enterprising neighbours climaxed in the St Brice's Day massacre of 3 November 1002, when Ethelred the Unready ordered the total slaughter of all Danes in England south of the Danelaw. It was the most terrible massacre ever seen in English history, comparable with the harrying of the North by William the Conqueror and to the 'ethnic cleansing' of more recent times. In retaliation, the Danish King Canute established his hold over the entire country in 1016, briefly uniting Britain to a European kingdom that included the whole of Scandinavia. It did not survive after his death, and, half a century later, the battle of Hastings swept away both Danish and Anglo-Saxon rule.

History is always on the side of the victors, and William of Normandy has had a good deal better press than he deserved, but, after the ruthless suppression of every vestige of native power, there was at least a settled and, for a while, unquestioned authority exercising control over the land and its people. William's desire to know the extent of his dubiously-acquired gains led to the most comprehensive survey of the population and material resources of the country before the advent of modern demography. Every man was quizzed about his family and his possessions and the details recorded. Not surprisingly, people thought it was a trial run for Doomsday. Not even the censuses of the 19th century ranged so widely in their extent and detail.

The machinations of Norman earls, as they rebelled against the king or sided with the losing party, led to events of great significance to them and their dependants, though life in the town had a tendency to continue much the same for ordinary citizens, irrespective of who lived in the castle. If the king took revenge, however, the effects might be disastrous for everyone, as in the year 1173 when the Earl of Leicester, far away in Normandy, rebelled against Henry II. As a consequence, the town was laid waste, and it has been argued that the relative absence of people in the north-eastern corner of Leicester, even up to the 19th century, was a consequence of the destruction wrought at this time.

A more probable explanation for the decline in Leicester's prosperity in these years has to do with developments in the cloth trade. In what historians refer to as 'the industrial revolution of the thirteenth century', fulling mills for the shrinking of woven wool were set up in areas such as the Cotswolds, where fast-flowing streams allowed the introduction of water-powered mills to drive the fulling stocks. Towns such as Leicester had no such source of power and the once-thriving local cloth industry migrated to new centres of manufacture. Whatever the reason, it is a fact that the north-eastern quarter of Leicester remained relatively uninhabited till the the mid-19th century.

Thirty years before the sack of Leicester, the abbey of St Mary de Pratis was established to the north of the town. It was here that the great servant of Henry VIII, Cardinal Wolsey, came to rest his weary bones in 1530. Had he returned to London there is little doubt that he would have met an even swifter end, but he was laid to rest in the Abbey, and his bones probably lie there to this day somewhere under the turf amid the neat outlines of the monastic ruin in Abbey Park.

About nine years later, the majestic nave and numerous other buildings were destroyed in the most comprehensive act of vandalism in our history. The roof-lead alone was valued at £1,000, an enormous sum at that time. All that remains of the abbey are the gatehouse, later incorporated into a residence known as Cavendish House, and the splendid wall built by

William Penny, who was abbot in the late 15th century.

As a principal residence of its medieval lords, Leicester saw a good many political events of national importance, and the great hall of the castle was the scene of several medieval parliaments. Henry V summoned two in Leicester, in 1414 and 1425. Simon de Montfort spent very little time here, though long enough to issue an edict, in 1255, expelling the Jews from the town. He pledged that 'no Jew or Jewess in my time, or in the time of any of my heirs, to the end of the world, shall inhabit, or remain, or obtain a residence in Leicester.' His action was a precursor to the later anti-semitism of Edward I, who drove the Jews out of York and thereafter expelled them from the whole of England.

After the death of Simon at the battle of Evesham in 1265, his lands were conferred on the younger son of the king, Edmund Crouchback, Earl of Lancaster. The nick-name apparently came from the cross which embellished his cloak and not from any physical deformity. In course of time the lands and title came to be held by John of Gaunt, who became Earl of Leicester in 1377. It was Gaunt who befriended the cleric, John Wycliffe, as Rector of Lutterworth. Wycliffe earned his soubriquet as 'the morning star of the Reformation' by translating the Bible into English and through his attack on the doctrine of trans-substantiation, the belief that the substance of the bread and wine of the communion service actually changes into the body and blood of Christ.

John of Gaunt's second wife was daughter of the King of Castille, Don Pedro the Cruel. To please her, Gaunt brought large numbers of singers and dancers from Spain, and it has been said that the Morris dance was thus introduced to England. Pedro was apparently so cruel that his disgruntled subjects overthrew him, and Gaunt was thus deprived of the inheritance he expected from his father-in-law. His third wife, Catherine Swynford, was a sister

4 *Cardinal Wolsey entering Leicester Abbey. One of the needlework designs of Mary Linwood. (See p.113)*

of the poet Geoffrey Chaucer, so it may well be that Leicester Castle was something of a Camelot in Gaunt's day, echoing to the *Canterbury Tales* as well as the songs of merry minstrels.

John of Gaunt died in 1399. He was only 59, not quite the 'time-honoured Lancaster' of Shakespeare's portrayal. After his death, when his son, Henry Bolingbroke, usurped Richard II and became Henry IV, his lands were absorbed into the royal estates.

Life was probably somewhat less eventful for the citizens of the town without a resident earl breathing down on them from the castle, and the burgesses were able to go about their business with somewhat greater freedom. In Elizabeth's reign, their independence from seignorial control was recognised in the town's charter granted in 1589, which allowed the merchants to buy and sell without paying dues to the lord of the manor.

Elizabeth's charter declared among other things: 'We therefore being graciously concerned for the improvement of the borough, and willing that for the future some certain and undoubted rule may be observed for maintaining the peace and good government of the people therein, and desiring that the borough may for ever remain peaceful and quiet, to the terror of evil-doers and the praise of them that do well, ... we order that the borough of Leicester shall be a free borough in itself, and that the burgesses and their successors for ever are and shall be by virtue of those presents one body corporate in fact and in name.'

5 *The Church at Lutterworth, from a series of sketches printed in the* Illustrated London News *to mark the 500th anniversary of Wycliffe's death in 1884.*

Two
AFTER BOSWORTH

If 1066 is the most remembered date in English history, then a close second must be the Battle of Bosworth in 1485, for it was here in Leicestershire that the Wars of the Roses ended in the death of Richard III. It was the final chapter in the long-running saga of conflicting claims to the throne by the houses of York and Lancaster. No one knew this at the time, for who could have foreseen that Richard was to be the last Yorkist to assert his claim as the true heir to the martyred Richard II?

There is a fine museum to the battle to the west of Market Bosworth with panoramic models of the field, where rival armies clashed. Some doubts have been expressed as to its precise location, but this decisive moment in English history has always been known as the Battle of Bosworth and is very definitely a Leicestershire event, though it was fought not far from the border with Warwickshire.

Richard has his passionate defenders even today and he clearly received unfair treatment at the hands of Shakespeare. The bard, after all, was a loyal subject of Henry Tudor's grand-daughter, Elizabeth, but there is no doubt that Richard was responsible for the elimination of William, Lord Hastings, the close friend of his brother, the late King Edward IV.

After Bosworth, Henry Tudor made no bones about who was in control. Over-mighty subjects were deprived of their personal armies and obliged to give up much of their wealth. In the ensuing peace there was little point in erecting fortified castles. Thus while Hastings' castle at Kirby Muxloe was moated, with gun-ports and a drawbridge, the family home of the Greys, built at Bradgate, three decades later, was a Tudor mansion. Both buildings were of brick, but Bradgate, set among the hills and craggy outcrops of Charnwood forest, was a testament to the stability born of Tudor despotism.

It was at Bradgate that Jane Grey spent her childhood. She was a grand-daughter of Elizabeth Woodville, the widow of Thomas Grey of Groby, who married Edward IV. Jane was next in line of succession after Henry VIII's own children and being born so close to the throne made her, inevitably, a pawn in the games men played for wealth and power. She was married off to the feckless Guildford Dudley in order to keep Mary Tudor from the throne. She did not seek to usurp: 'The crown is not my right, the Lady Mary is the rightful Queen,' she protested, but circumstances made her the figurehead of Protestant opposition to the Catholic Mary and she was punished for the sins of power-hungry men.

With hindsight, those who foresaw a return to Rome need have had no fear, for Mary died childless, and the Protestant revolution was confirmed by the reign of Elizabeth. Twenty years after the dissolution it was inconceivable that the Church would be repossessed of its lands.

The passing of the monasteries brought an end to the effective relief of the poor by the Church, and the closure of such labour-intensive institutions in the county as Garendon Abbey, Croxton Abbey, the nunnery of Grace Dieu and priories of Ulverscroft, Launde and Owston must have caused much grief and misery. Added to this would be the loss of support and income generated by the town's own priories of Grey Friars and White Friars and by the fabulously rich college of St Mary de Castro.

Some owners of former church property may have required more labour in order to exploit their extended estates, but many would have taken their cue from wealthy farmers who were consolidating their land-holdings into

6 *The Gatehouse of Kirby Muxloe Castle, much the same today as it was when building ceased in 1483, after the execution of Hastings. Contrast this moated medieval castle with the picturesque ruins of Bradgate House, the home of Lady Jane Grey, built a generation later, which makes no attempt at fortification.*

10 / Leicestershire Events

7 *Bradgate House. The chapel and ruined tower as it is today.*

8 *Portrait of Lady Jane Grey, from Nichols'* History of Leicestershire, *(1791).*

manageable fields in order to meet the demand for wool. This was the motivation for much of the early enclosure movement when individual holdings in the ancient open fields were put together into privately owned tracts. Peasant farmers frequently lost what independence they had and were obliged to seek a living as hired hands or to swell the numbers of roaming beggars. Furthermore, sheep farming required a minimal labour force compared with the growing of crops, so that unemployment was a recurrent problem for Tudor and Stuart monarchs.

Enclosure of the ancient arable fields sometimes came about through the ravages of plague and was sometimes in response to the gradual decline of population which made labour-intensive agriculture difficult to sustain. Whatever the cause, there would be some peasant farmers who were no longer able to live and work on the land and who were therefore obliged to seek for a living elsewhere. They may have been absorbed into neighbouring towns or other villages, but others had recourse to begging and swelled the numbers of vagrants, to the terror of wealthier citizens, who were doubtless as puzzled by their presence as we are by the appearance of asylum-seekers in search of a better life today.

9 *Ulverscroft Priory, sketched by Mrs F. F. Palmer. It was founded in A.D. 1130 and spared in 1536 but dissolved with the other monasteries in 1539.*

10 *Great Stretton Church as it is today. As often happened, domestic buildings collapsed and became irregular mounds within the pattern of ridge and furrow, only the house of God bearing witness to the existence of a once-thriving community.*

>Hark, Hark the dogs do bark,
>The beggars are come to town.
>Some gave them white bread and some gave them brown
>And some took a horse-whip and drove them from town.

When we consider the human repercussions of uprooting families from their homesteads and turning them loose without any compensation in order to convert arable land into sheep pastures, these enclosures must be regarded as events of shattering importance.

The church is all that remains of Great Stretton to the south of the Roman road which ran from Leicester to Colchester. Successive outbreaks of plague probably reduced the once thriving township till it was uneconomic to farm the open fields, and it was turned over to sheep farming. By contrast the neighbouring settlement of Little Stretton still survives as a viable hamlet.

W.G. Hoskins wrote of this period: 'The country gentlemen of Leicestershire, a small county in which everybody of some social position knew everybody else, and in which there was a great deal of inter-marriage, were not slow to learn from each other the new way of doubling their incomes by turning their estates into sheep and cattle pastures, and driving away their tenants from the one-time arable fields.' (W.G. Hoskins, *Essays in Leicestershire History*, Liverpool UP, 1950)

In the century that followed the death of Elizabeth, Leicestershire witnessed its share of historic events. George Villiers, handsome young favourite of James I, was born at Brooksby and lived at Goadby Marwood. He went to France to finish his education and on his return he caught the eye of King James, at once becoming the royal favourite. He was made a knight of the Garter and Viscount Villiers in 1616 and became Earl of Buckingham in 1617. The following year he was created a Marquis and in 1623 he was created Duke of Buckingham. Charles I doted on him even more than his

11 *The Church and Hall at Goadby Marwood north of Melton Mowbray. The Hall is of mid-18th-century date, long after the time of George Villiers, but certainly there when Edmund Cartwright, the inventor of the power loom, was rector from 1779.*

12 *The church and hall at Staunton Harold as illustrated in Nichols'* History of Leicestershire.

father had done. But if the king's infatuation seemed limitless, the patience of his subjects was not. Buckingham was assassinated, to the chagrin of Charles and the relief of everybody else, at Portsmouth in 1628.

According to the historian John Nichols, Buckingham's early schooling was at Billesdon and it was here, again according to Nichols, that the Quaker, George Fox, also went to school. Born in 1624, Fox exemplifies the religious turmoil of the Commonwealth period. From his home in Fenny Drayton on the southern border of the county, he traversed the length and breadth of the country inspiring his followers with a conviction that God could be experienced directly without the need for priests and prelates. It was a revolution too far for most moderate Englishmen, and the fear of religious extremists, like the Quakers, goes some way to explain the restoration of monarchy in 1660.

Among those loyal to the king during the Civil War was Sir Robert Shirley at Staunton Harold. His refusal to compromise led to his imprisonment in the Tower where he died at the age of 29. During his short life, he began the building of a beautiful gothic church, standing in the grounds of Staunton Harold hall, which his successor adorned with the defiant inscription: 'When all things sacred were throughout ye nation either demolished or profaned Sir Robert Shirley Baronet founded this Church whose singular praise it is to have done ye best of things in ye worst of times And hoped them in the most calamitous. The Righteous shall be had in everlasting remembrance.' Nikolaus Pevsner describes the house and chapel of Staunton Harold as 'unsurpassed in the country', especially when seen from across the lakes.

It was during this century, when political and religious differences tore the country apart, that the hosiery trade first made its appearance in Leicestershire. Stockings had long been knitted by hand and continued to be so made, but the stocking frame, which was destined to become the cornerstone of local industrial activity over the next three hundred years, first made its appearance in Hinckley in 1640. During the early 18th century, the new industry was based mainly in London under the control of the London Company of Framework Knitters but, in regulating the trade to the benefit of their own members, the guild made the prospect of moving away from the metropolis more attractive to the master hosiers. Consequently, the predominance of London in hosiery manufacture declined and the East Midlands, where the industry had its origin and where cheaper labour was obtainable, became its main location.

13   *The stockinger.*

By the mid-18th century, several threads in the fabric of local history began to stand out more clearly and we can look at them as separate clusters of events in the following chapters. Disasters such as flood, fire and storm feature in this story as do crimes and the impact of wars, but there are also the happier events, celebrating the coming of kings and queens or the triumph of some local sporting celebrity. But firstly, let us take a look at some of the events surrounding the dominant dynasties of Leicestershire.

Three
NOBILITY AND NOTORIETY

Leicestershire has its full complement of ancient families, but its history was dominated to a great extent by two of these, the Hastings and the Greys. As the name suggests, an ancestor of the Hastings family came over with William of Normandy. By 1364 they owned land at Wistow and were lords of the manor of Braunstone. They acquired lands and titles elsewhere and, by the mid-15th century, William Hastings had risen to be the most powerful magnate in the land. He married the king's sister and became Baron Hastings, Steward of the Honor of Leicester and Constable of the Castle, with numerous other offices of profit. He demonstrated his loyalty to Edward IV in 1470 when he raised an army to defeat the Earl of Warwick at the battle of Barnet, so restoring Edward to his throne.

All this made him far too close to Edward and his sons, the Princes in the Tower, to endear him to their uncle Richard. Hastings was consequently arrested at a council meeting and condemned and executed in May 1483, within a month of Edward's death. According to Sir Thomas More, he was 'brought forth into the green beside the chapel within the Tower and his head laid down upon a log of timber and there stricken off.' His widow lived on in the gatehouse of Kirby Castle, but his descendants lived for the most part at Ashby Castle and later at Castle Donington.

Richard may have had a rather more legitmate claim to the throne than has generally been acknowledged. According to the television presenter, Tony Robinson, records in the cathedral of Rouen discovered by Dr Michael Jones, confirm Richard's contention that his brother was the illegitimate offspring of a liaison between his mother and an English archer. In Shakespeare's play, Richard asserts:

> When that my mother went with child
> Of that insatiate Edward, noble York
> My princely father then had wars in France
> And, by true computation of the time,
> Found that the issue was not his begot;
> Which well appeared in his lineaments,
> Being nothing like the noble Duke my father.

14 *Ashby Castle today.*

It is a fact that both Edward IV and Henry VIII were uncommonly tall and well-built, in contrast to the general run of English kings; the archer's son evidently passed his genes to Henry via his daughter, Elizabeth of York.

If the royal line was illegitimate, then the true descent should have followed from the offspring of the Duke of Clarence, whose grand-daughter, Catherine, married Francis Hastings, and, according to this view, the rightful kings of England would have traced their descent through the Leicestershire family at Ashby-de-la-Zouch.

Be that as it may, with the change in political winds after Bosworth, the Hastings were restored to favour. William Lord Hastings' grandson, George, was created Earl of Huntingdon and, during the reign of Elizabeth, Henry Hastings, the 3rd Earl of Huntingdon, was one of her most influential subjects. It was he who greatly increased the Wyggeston Hospital foundation and that of the hospital in the Newarke. Part of his town house, the Huntingdon Tower, survived until the widening of Leicester High Street in 1902.

During the Civil War, the 6th Earl managed to keep aloof from politics, but several of his relatives took opposing sides. Henry Hastings, the younger of Huntingdon's sons, stoutly defended the king and became the most effective military commander in the midlands, bringing much needed courage and daring to the royal campaigns; in recognition of which, he was made Baron Loughborough in 1643.

Henry Hastings' brother, Ferdinando, was firmly on the side of Parliament, as were the Earl of Stamford and the rest of the Grey family with Sir Edward

15 *Breaches in the Town Walls made by royalist troops during the Civil War as illustrated in John Nichols'* History of the County of Leicestershire.

The captions to these engravings read: 'Breaches in the South Newarke Wall, hastily repaired after the Siege' and 'Embrasure and Sallyport in the garden of Thomas Dabbs Esq. Newarke'.

Hartopp, Sir Arthur Hazelrigg of Noseley and his brother, Archdale Palmer. Both Thomas Grey and Hazelrigg later became signatories to the King's death warrant.

One of the first actions of the Earl of Stamford, at the start of the Civil War in June 1642, was to remove the arms and ammunition from Leicester to the safety of his house at Bradgate. Six weeks later, Henry Hastings and Prince Rupert led a royalist attack on Bradgate retrieving the arms and taking much else besides. The Greys fortunately escaped with their lives. This skirmish was followed by a more serious confrontation at Market Harborough, a few days later, when Rupert's men suffered a reverse. Needing provisions for his cavalry, he ordered an attack upon the hay crop which had been delivered to the town. The royalist force of about 1,000 men was surprised and ambushed by a troop belonging to the Earl of Stamford, and Rupert was forced to flee towards Rockingham, leaving the dead and all his booty behind.

Two weeks after this, while stationed at Queniborough, Rupert sent a letter to the Mayor of Leicester demanding £2,000 toward the royalist cause. Representations on behalf of the Mayor and Aldermen led the king to rescind the order, but not before Prince Rupert had taken £500 from the Corporation. Not surprisingly, the sympathies of the town remained with Parliament throughout the Civil War. But its military protection was defective, and Rupert was able to inflict a crushing defeat on the town in 1645.

On 30 May, the parliamentary garrison at Leicester found itself outnumbered ten to one by troops loyal to the king. Rupert's forces bombarded the town walls from their encampment at Raw Dykes and, after a day and night of fierce fighting, the town succumbed. Hastings was appointed governor of Leicester and he was given the task of destroying much of the town defences in order to strengthen what remained.

Opinions differ as to the degree of severity meted out by Prince Rupert, but according to the royalist historian, Clarendon, 'the conquerors pursued their advantage with the usual licence of rapine and plunder and miserably sacked the whole town without any distinction of persons or places. Churches and hospitals, as well as the houses, were made a prey to the greedy soldiers, to the exceeding regret of the king.' 140 cart-loads of plunder were carried off to the king at Newark, including the seal and maces of the Corporation.

16 *The Siege of Leicester, 1645, as illustrated in John Nichols.*

During the siege, King Charles had lodged in the house of the Countess of Devonshire in the ruins of Leicester Abbey. On 4 June 1645, he stayed a night at Wistow Hall, the home of Sir Richard Halford, a staunch Royalist who had been imprisoned in the tower of London in 1640. The royalist headquarters was at Market Harborough where a council of war was held on 12 June. Two days later, near the village of Naseby, Charles suffered a decisive defeat. After the battle he made for Ashby, calling en route at Wistow where he and Prince Rupert swapped their own ornate saddles and bridles for plainer ones. They never returned to claim them.

Though Naseby inflicted a mortal blow it did not end the war, and royalist forces held out at Belvoir Castle for another six months. Phillip Scaysbrook, in his masterly and gripping account of *The Civil War in Leicestershire and Rutland*, gives the text of a message sent to the royalist garrison at Belvoir by the parliamentary force at Grantham. The spelling and punctuation have been modernised.

> Sir,
> We are sent down and authorised by the two houses of parliament, to use our best endeavours for finishing this bloody internecine war, wherewith this kingdom hath been now for some time afflicted. And in pursuance of that duty, we do hereby in their names, demand of you that you surrender up into our hands the castle of Belvoir for their use. We do further let you know the pious care of parliament to prevent, as far as possibly may be, the effusion of Christian blood and the destruction of towns and castles and houses in this Kingdom, and accordingly are willing to entertain a treaty with you. Whereunto we shall only add that if you refuse or neglect the mercy of the parliament at this time, while it may be had, and flatter yourself with vain hopes that you may obtain as good and honourable conditions hereafter as at present, we do most unfeinedly assure you, you will utterly deceive yourself. Beside we think good to advertize you that it is not the part of a soldier, nor of a wise man, to endeavour the holding of a place not tenable, when there are not the least hopes of being relieved. Which act in you will by all men be interpreted rather an affected obstinacy than a soldierly resolution. Consider likewise seriously with yourself, that the exposing so many Christians, as are now under your command, to manifest destruction, will undoubtedly be required of you. We will expect your answer by 8 of the clock tomorrow morning.

It is signed by Rutland and five others.

After much deliberation this plea for common sense was accepted, and Colonel Lucas led his men out of Belvoir. Beneath the chivalry of the letter was doubtless a desire on Rutland's part not to lay waste his own castle. A few days later the garrison at Ashby also fell, and, in the following June, the Civil War ended as the King surrendered at Newark in Nottinghamshire.

Lord Loughborough's prominent support for the King led to hefty fines as the pendulum of war swung in favour of Parliament, and property had to be sold to meet debts. The original Hastings estate at Braunstone was sold to James Winstanley in 1649 and remained with the same family till the 20th century. A fine new mansion was built in 1775 in what is now Braunstone Park.

By the late 18th century, the Hastings family was facing a crisis through its failure to produce a male heir. Theophilus, the 9th earl, had married Selina Shirley, a lady of singular devotion who was so moved by the teachings of John Wesley that she began her very own church, known as the Countess of Huntingdon's Connexion. Her prime intention was to spread the blessings of Methodism to the upper reaches of society instead of directing its attention solely to the downtrodden masses. Selina's piety may have had something to do with a troubled conscience, for she had cheated her distant relations out of a fortune.

17 Braunstone Hall from the illustration in John Nichols.

The saga of her misdeeds began in 1789 when her son, the 10th earl, died. The countess, knowing that the title and lands should then have passed to a descendant of the 2nd earl, resolved to keep the family fortune in her own hands as far as possible. Paget and Irvine, in their *History of Leicestershire*, tell the story thus: 'when she heard that the Rev. Theophilus Hastings was laying claim to the title, she and Lady Loudon, her grand-daughter-in-law, proceeded to make sure he would get nothing else. She sent for all the settlements and deeds and did nothing to prevent Lady Loudon from destroying all those which tended to prove that the property followed the title. When the family lawyer tried to restrain her, Lady Loudon clung to the precious deed she was destroying till it burnt her hand.' Repentance came over the Countess of Loudon before her death and she ordered that the hand which had so offended should be cut off and buried in the park at Donington—but not till after her death.

Some twenty years later, a chance encounter with a former servant in the Hastings household led a lawyer, Henry Nugent-Bell, who was interested in the case, to set about restoring the Huntingdon peerage to the rightful heir.

As a result, Hans Francis Hastings, descendant of the 2nd Earl, who was at one time thought to be drowned off the coast of Cork, was welcomed into the House of Lords in 1819 as the 11th Earl of Huntingdon. The romantic story of the young and relatively poor adventurer returning to his ancestral home as the rightful earl evidently caught the popular imagination.

As the new earl entered Castle Donington the bells rang and a band played and the lads and lasses danced through the evening till the small hours. Nugent-Bell tells the story of his triumphant return and of an encounter with a childhood acquaintance:

> In the course of the evening many persons from the neighbourhood of Belton who had been his playmates, when a boy, requested to have the honour of seeing him, and among the rest an old tenant who, in his Lordship's infantile days, had been a special favourite. This man was introduced, and his Lordship, instantly recognising him, shook him good-naturedly and unceremoniously by the hand. Honest Hodge, somewhat confused, stared for a considerable time at his former but long-forgotten acquaintance and at last told him he did not recollect him and that he had his doubts if he were Master Frank, the youngest son of Colonel George Hastings. 'What!' said his Lordship, with that frankness and unaffected good humour peculiar to him, 'is it possible you can forget me? I am sure I remember you very well, and I perfectly remember the day we were skating together on the Horse Pond at the back of Billy Toone's house, in Belton, when I tumbled you into the hole made for the cows to drink from and then gave you a penny and my new pair of Christmas gloves, not to tell or cry.' 'Ah! By God! You are Master Frank sure enough!' exclaimed the delighted farmer, whose recollection was awakened by the circumstance, and whose dilated features broadly evinced his satisfaction at the discovery. His Lordship desired him to get his dinner, and then to toast the hand that ducked him in the horse-pond, till he was drunk as an emperor, which liberty the worthy fellow hastened to avail himself of.

Though he visited Castle Donington, the new earl did not live there, for Selina, the religious countess, had succeeded in keeping most of the family wealth in the hands of her immediate descendants. Her son-in-law became the Earl of Moira and her grandson, a Governor General of India. After his death, in 1826, his son George married Barbara Grey, thus uniting the two families that had so long been rivals. But the fortune so jealously guarded was frittered away by their son, the 4th and last Marquis of Hastings. His downfall was horse racing and he died, in 1868, worn out at the age of twenty-six. Donington Hall, built by his grandfather, lay empty for many years and became a P.O.W. camp in the First world War. Between the wars, it was turned into a motor racing club house, and the park became a race track.

Meanwhile, the restored Earl of Huntingdon's family lived in Ireland for many years before returning to Leicestershire. The 15th Earl became Minister of Agriculture in Clement Attlee's Labour government of 1945. His successor, the present bearer of the title, lives in Berkshire.

The Grey family enjoyed a more peaceful existence at Bradgate, though their story was not uneventful. After the death of Lady Jane Grey, the family

18 Plaque in Bradgate Park.

suffered something of a decline, but in the next century Henry Grey became Baron Grey of Groby and 1st Earl of Stamford.

Jane's widowed mother, the Duchess of Suffolk, later married her groom. Adrian Stokes was fifteen years her junior and such a mesalliance inevitably caused comment. 'Has the woman so far forgotten herself as to marry a common groom?' asked the astonished Queen Elizabeth. Whatever the world may have thought, the couple seem to have enjoyed a happy life together at nearby Beaumanor.

Bradgate itself seems to have been lived in till the early 18th century and was visited by King William in 1694. In an age which had not yet discovered beauty in rugged unspoiled country, the house must have seemed remote and uncongenial to a young woman used to the social life of London. It was in a mood of distaste for her new home that the wife of the 2nd earl complained in a letter to her sister that the house was tolerable, that the country was a forest, and that the inhabitants were all brutes. She then seems to have acted upon her sister's sympathetic suggestion that she should 'set fire to the house and run away by the light of it'. Not too much damage was done to the building, but aristocratic arson was not conducive to marital harmony, and the earl and his wife separated shortly afterwards.

From 1739 the old house at Bradgate was bricked up and left to decay. From this time until 1772 the Grey family lived in their house at Enville in Staffordshire. In that year the 5th Earl Stamford and his wife moved to Dunham Massey in Cheshire. The old home in Bradgate park became the picturesque ruin we see today.

Although the Greys no longer lived there, visitors were generally allowed to wander over the park and it became a favourite recreation ground for

19 *John Henry, 5th Duke of Rutland, from the* Illustrated London News, *1857*.

Leicester people. The fact that the public can still walk at will in Bradgate is due to the remarkable generosity of Charles Bennion, a local industrialist, who bought the estate from the last Grey owner in 1928 and gave it to the people of Leicestershire the following day.

With the declining influence of the Grey and Hastings families, the dominant political power in the county was exercised by the Manners dynasty at Belvoir. The manor of Belvoir had been in the possession of the family since the 15th century, and the Earldom of Rutland was conferred on them in 1525. In 1703, Queen Anne granted the titles of Marquis of Granby and Duke of Rutland. The almost feudal respect and veneration in which the Manners family came to be held is reflected in the prominence given to his statue in Leicester Market Place. He held the dukedom for 70 years and the office of Lord Lieutenant for more than fifty of these.

At Coleorton Hall to the west of Whitwick, Sir George Beaumont gathered round him a coterie of artistic friends among whom was the poet Wordsworth and the painter John Constable, though, for some curious reason, Beaumont took a dislike to J.M.W. Turner. The Beaumonts had owned Coleorton for nearly four hundred years, when Sir George re-built the hall in Gothic style in 1805. The Jacobean playwright Francis Beaumont is commemorated in one of several verses penned by Wordsworth to be found on monuments in the grounds. Sir George was a painter of some note and he donated much of his own collection, which included works by Rubens, Rembrandt and Reynolds, to the newly formed National Gallery.

20 *Statue in Leicester Market Place.*

21 *Coleorton Hall built in 1805 for Sir George Beaumont, a patron of the arts and friend of William Wordsworth. For many years it was a regional headquarters of the National Coal Board, but it is now divided into luxury apartments in private ownership.*

Four
Fox Hunting

22 Pork pies have been made in Melton for nearly two hundred years. Her Majesty Queen Elizabeth is seen here at the last remaining pie factory in Melton during a royal visit to the town in 1996.

Perhaps the activity most widely associated with Leicestershire is the sport of fox-hunting. In medieval times the fox was regarded as vermin to be killed rather than hunted. When it was first used as a quarry for huntsmen at the end of the 17th century, it was not chased by gentlemen of fashion. This was because its speed made it impossible for ordinary hounds to overtake it and, consequently, if John Peel were to succeed, he had to be up at the break of day when the fox was still tired after its nocturnal hunt for food and with its stomach full enough to impede escape. No self-respecting gentleman would think of rising in the small hours to hunt, and so fox-hunting remained the preserve of small farmers and the lesser gentry.

It was Hugo Meynell of Quorn Hall who revolutionised hunting after he came to Leicestershire in 1753. He was wealthy and ambitious and he set about transforming the sport by selective breeding of hounds. Once the dogs were able to keep up with the fox, hunting could attract men of social standing, who would not have to rise from their beds unduly early to enjoy a day in the saddle. Thus it was Meynell, who became the arbiter of fashion in fox-hunting, and it was due to his presence at Quorn that the sport became focused here in Leicestershire.

Quorn itself was too small to cater for all the demands of the hunting fraternity and, while Loughborough benefited briefly as the nearest town of any size, it was Melton Mowbray that soon became the acknowledged centre of the fox-hunting universe. Melton was well placed to enable visitors to participate in the hunting activities of the Duke of Rutland at Belvoir and of the Earl of Gainsborough at Cottesmore, the Fernie Hunt, which developed out of Meynell's own pack at Quorn, and the Atherstone hounds. Queen Victoria visited Belvoir in 1843, and Prince Albert took part in a hunt in which three foxes were run to ground and killed.

It may well be asked why the county should have retained its pre-eminence as the centre of hunting, since many other districts provide equally attractive landscapes and just as many foxes. Perhaps one reason is the absence of great landed estates over which the trampling of crops and fences would not be

23 *Workers in the yard of Tebbutt's Pork Pie factory, about 1895.*

24 *Advertisement for pork pies.*

25 *The First Stilton Cheese Fair in Sherard Street, Melton Mowbray in 1883.*

26 *A fox hunter enjoying a Melton pork pie.*

welcome. Leicestershire gentry were generally keen to enjoy the sport and the predominance of pastoral farming reduced the inconvenience of the chase to agriculture. 'Among those who built or owned lodges in Melton as headquarters for hunting were the Earl of Wilton, the Marquis of Hastings, the Countess of Warwick, the Duke and Duchess of Cleveland, the Earl of Plymouth, the Marquis of Worcester and the Maharanee of Cooch Behar.' (Brian Bailey, p.127)

Gentlemen a-hunting need sustenance, and what better way to dine in the open air than on Melton Mowbray pork pie and Stilton cheese? Both these delicacies have their origin in Leicestershire and gained popularity in part from their convenience as food to be taken to the chase and the grouse moors. It is the retention of juices from the meat cooked into the pastry case that gives Melton pies their succulent flavour, and a good pork pie will keep fresh much longer than sandwiches.

The young aristocrats drawn to Leicestershire by the lure of fox-hunting often saw themselves as above the law and none demonstrated this with more panache than the Marquis of Waterford. According to Brian Bailey, 'At Lowesby Hall, he amused himself by shooting the eyes out of all the portraits on the walls, and for a wager of a hundred guineas, brought his favourite horse indoors and jumped a five-barred gate in the dining-room.' On another occasion 'he put a donkey in an unsuspecting victim's bed and painted aniseed on the heels of a clergyman's horse and set bloodhounds

27 *'Painting the Town Red'*

after him.' He and his inebriated companions went out one night in 1837 and daubed Melton's *White Swan Inn* with red paint. While humbler lads would have been transported or hung for such blatant vandalism, these rakes go down in history as the first to 'paint the town red'.

Evidently, the Marquis was not alone in seeking more than the usual equestrian thrill of the chase. Another set of huntsmen with a taste for nocturnal excitement are depicted in this drawing of the mid-night hunt. The instigator of this particular piece of high-class idiocy was a woman, Lady Augusta Fane, who, in 1890, 'invited her guests to take part in a midnight steeplechase over a course lit by railway lamps, and wearing ladies' night-dresses over their hunting gear.' (Bailey 128)

Whatever view we take of fox-hunting, there is no doubt that it once held an almost mystical place in the lives of country folk. No one pretended that its purpose was to destroy vermin; on the contrary, foxes were encouraged in Leicestershire in order to provide the necessary quarry, and many a copse today owes its origin to the fox-coverts deliberately planted for them. Hunting became an obsession with generations of wealthy farmers and landowners.

FOX HUNTING / 31

28 *The Midnight Hunt.*

29 *Huntsmen were clearly a law unto themselves. At Whissendine station, Edmondthorpe, on 20 March 1879, the Cottesmore Hunt ignored the pleas of a crossing keeper, and attempted to make a short cut along the railway, with disastrous results.*

32 / LEICESTERSHIRE EVENTS

30 *At Hoby water-mill, in February 1874, several gentlemen attempted to cross a plank bridge and discovered their mistake when they fell into the River Wreake.*

31 *Not all huntsmen and women are so reckless. Here we see the Fernie hounds gathering at Wistow in 1927.*

32 *It was hunting that brought the Prince of Wales to Leicestershire, in 1932, and here that he first met Wallis Simpson. The Prince of Wales and Mrs Simpson photographed at Craven Lodge when in Leicestershire for the races in 1935.*

It was the touchstone of social respectability, and those unfortunate enough to have made their money in the town were often lured into the county to enjoy the prestige of joining the fox-hunting fraternity.

If gentlemen and their wives rode to hounds, their servants and labourers often owed their livelihood to gratifying this collective craving. Ostlers, grooms, blacksmiths, stable-boys and those breeding and caring for the hounds were far out-numbered by the shop-keepers and hoteliers catering for visitors in the season, and the gardeners and domestic servants, who depended on the aristocratic owners of hunting-lodges.

33 *The Prince of Wales, the future Edward VIII, riding to hounds.*

It is all very different today. The thrill of the chase is now more likely to involve hunt saboteurs protesting against 'the unspeakable in pursuit of the uneatable', than watching the actual tearing to pieces of one terrified creature by a ravenous pack of dogs.

Five
LEICESTERSHIRE AT LEISURE

If we look beyond fox-hunting to the wider field of sport and entertainment the task of selecting 'events' becomes much more difficult, for every boxing match and game of football would count as an event to the participants and spectators. Action-shots of actual events, however, are rare. There can be few photographs more boring than the posed pictures of the school hockey or rugger team, unless, of course, you recall being there or find amusement in the sporting garb of past generations.

In medieval times, annual trade fairs provided a welcome diversion from the daily routine as jugglers, merry-go rounds and fortune tellers latched on to the fringes of the commercial activity that was the primary business of such fairs.

Shakespeare makes reference to the fair at Hinckley in *Henry IV Part 2*, when the servant of Justice Shallow asks his master: 'Do you mean to stop any of William's wages about the sack he lost the other day at Hinckley fair?' Ultimately, the festive activities became the fair itself, as with Nottingham's Goose Fair, and the exchange of merchandise took place elsewhere. Leicester retained its fair in Humberstone Gate till 1904, when the needs of traffic were seen as more important than just having fun.

There was an element of puritanical disapproval of such unbridled entertainment at the fairs. Certainly, the distaste for rough lower-class entertainment played a part in the abolition of Whipping Toms in 1846.

The Whipping Toms were young men who traditionally appeared in the Newarke, in Leicester, on Shrove Tuesdays carrying wagon whips with which they attacked the lower legs of anyone passing through the area at mid-day. The rector of St Mary's thought himself immune from such attentions till he learned his mistake the hard way and had to take to his heels. The religious origin of such 'shriving' or purging of sins at Lent had long-since degenerated into an excuse for horse-play, and the respectable citizens of the neighbourhood were understandably anxious to crush the practice. Consequently, a clause in the Improvement Act of 1846 declared the practice illegal, and when the local lads assembled the following year to have a game of football instead, this too was disallowed

34 *The last fair in Humberstone Gate, in 1904.*

by constables of the newly-created police force, the guardians of middle-class morality.

Fortunately for us, the county had not such a puritanical attitude and an equally ancient and unruly mob was allowed to rampage over the fields of Hallaton, close to the borders of Rutland and Northamptonshire, every Easter Monday. Hallaton's 'bottle-kicking' is probably as close as one gets to the origin of modern football. The villages of Medbourne and Hallaton compete against each other to get three 'bottles' or wooden casks across several fields. Victory goes to the side that takes two of the three 'bottles' over a brook that divides the two parishes. There is no limit to the number of participants and no rules as to what is or is not allowed.

The site now known as Hare-Pie Bank was probably venerated in pre-Roman times and a holy well located on the hill later became the site of a chapel dedicated to St Morrel. To this must be added the legend concerning two local ladies saved by a hare. The hare ran across the path of a bull and so diverted its attention from the two women. In gratitude, they gave the rents of land known as 'Hare Crop Leys' to the rector, on condition that he provided annually two hare pies, two dozen loaves and a quantity of ale to the villagers, every Easter Monday. In addition, he was required to preach a sermon and offer a service. All this is confirmed in John Nichols' *History*, published in 1791, and it explains the peculiar terms of the Enclosure Award of the same year, which specifically required the rector to provide hare pies and penny loaves to the villagers, in return for his tenure of the Hare Crop Leys.

The Bottle-kicking itself may well be of ancient origin and it probably grew out of a customary gathering on the hillside, when young men demonstrated their athletic skills. Similar gatherings are said to have been held on Burrough Hill and at Dane Hills to the west of Leicester. Often these events would be held on Shrove Tuesday, as was the case with the Whipping Toms in The Newarke. At Hallaton, all the festivities occur on Easter Monday, which may well suggest an origin dating from the pagan worship of Oestre, the goddess of fertility, symbolised by the sacred hare. That the vicinity was seen to have religious significance is evident from the discovery of the gold and silver coin hoard mentioned in chapter one.

Several hundred people gather in Hallaton every year and the annual event begins with a march-past of local bands through the village street. This is followed, at about mid-day, with the blessing, by the vicar, of an enormous hare pie on the steps of the parish church. The vicar then breaks up the pie and scatters some of it into the crowd. The rest of the pie is placed in two sacks to be eaten later.

Everyone then moves to the butter-cross, where the vicar blesses the 'bottles' and ties them with red and white ribbon. The bottles are three specially-made wooden casks bound with iron hoops, two of which contain beer, the third being a dummy. Penny loaves of bread are then distributed, no doubt once relished by the poor as a welcome addition to the larder. Then it's time for refreshment, at one of the excellent local pubs, before the entire populace moves off for the start of the Scrambling and Bottle-kicking. This is on Hare Pie Bank, a field above the village, set aside for the purpose under the Enclosure Act of 1770, though long pre-dating that Act as the customary location.

At Hare Pie Bank, two sacks containing the pie are swung round above the heads of the crowd before the contents are released, again allowing an unseemly scramble for tasty morsels to be consumed, with any luck, before they fall to the ground. The Bottle-kicking itself is a pitched battle in which

35 *Bottle-kicking in 1993. Rather like a gigantic rugby scrum in which the ball, or 'bottle', emerges, periodically, in the possession of one side or the other.*

all the young men of Hallaton pit their strength against that of young men from the neighbouring village of Medbourne.

The winning team is the first to cross the village boundaries with two of the three bottles. There are absolutely no rules and no referee. Nor is there any barrier between the participants and the on-lookers, so anyone is likely to be drawn into the mêlée and only the nimble-footed venture close to the action. Despite the name of the game, kicking is the last thing one would be tempted to do with a heavy iron-bound wooden barrel. Instead, the bottles are thrown, carried and rolled while contestants fight, wrestle, push and shove one another in a gigantic rugby scrum. It's all great fun, and no one is surprised if a few bones are broken in the course of the day.

It is said that when the parson at Hallaton attempted, in 1790, to put an end to such uncivilised and possibly pagan behaviour, he found the slogan: 'No pie, no parson, and a job for the glazier' chalked over the church doors and walls.

A parson of very different mettle was William Hanbury of Church Langton. He was one of those enterprising individuals who not only had business acumen and an enormous capacity for hard work, but also possessed a vision of how to make the world a better place. He came to Church Langton in 1749 with a keen interest in botany and, in order to find suitable trees for planting on his land, he set up his own horticultural business. He even published two books on gardening and forestry. So great was his success in selling trees that he was able to establish his own trust to provide work, almshouses and hospitals for the poor. He also drew up plans for the creation of a new university and a vast cathedral, with a spire higher than that of Salisbury, to be built on his land.

Alas, Hanbury died early and his grandiose schemes never materialised, but his charity still exists and he deserves to be remembered

36 *More action at the bottle-kicking in 1993. There simply are no rules.*

37 *Ten years on, in 2003, the hairstyles and gear may have changed, but the content is just as unruly.*

for the lavish musical festival he inaugurated in 1759. Originally conceived as an advertising gimmick to increase the sales of his plants and seeds, it was a huge success. Hanbury engaged a full London orchestra, installed a new organ, put up galleries for the occasion and provided refreshments in a great dining booth.

This was the first time that Handel's *Messiah* was performed in a church and it was a sell-out. Hanbury wrote that 'stable room, beds and lodgings were bespoke at Harborough and almost every village … The inns and even alehouses were soon full, and the *Swan* at Harborough made 30 beds out of their own house. The Duke of Devonshire was obliged to lodge at a tradesman's.' Three years later he arranged an 'oratorio season for the nobility and gentry' of Leicestershire held in St Martin's church. This time it included *Judas Maccabeus* and *Samson* as well as *Messiah*.

Another man to make musical history in Leicester was William Gardiner, a composer of many popular songs and hymns. Gardiner is best known for his book entitled *Music and Friends*, published in 1838, but he was instrumental in arranging several great music festivals in the town.

During the French Revolution many asylum-seekers from the continent settled in England, and one of these found refuge at Great Dalby where he made the acquaintance of Gardiner. It was through this friendship that the music of Beethoven first came to England. Some years later, in 1848, Gardiner was on holiday in Bonn when a statue to Beethoven was unveiled. He was invited to sign the parchment scroll, which was ceremonially placed in the base of the statue, and the only space available on which to sign was that beneath the names of Victoria and Albert. It was, said Gardiner, the proudest day of his life.

St Margaret's pasture, to the north of Leicester, seems to have been the venue of all manner of sports and pastimes. It was here that horse races were held prior to 1742. Racing thereafter took place on the fields to the south of the town and from 1802 when the South Fields were enclosed, it was located on what is now Victoria Park, for two days a year, always on a Thursday and Friday. Then in 1883 the event was moved to a new course at Oadby. It was not a popular move.

The Leicester Race Week had always been something of an annual holiday with fireworks, bands, singers, dancing as well as cock-fighting at *The Saracen's Head* and plays at the Assembly Rooms. It was Leicester's main annual holiday, a 'yearly break in the monotony of daily life', 'the great carnival of the year' and workers saved up their overtime so as to enjoy it. The races drew together aristocrats like the Duke of Rutland with the ordinary people of town and county. In 1863 the *Leicester Journal* observed that 'it is said that Epsom is a meeting for the masses, and Goodwood for the gentry: Leicester may enjoy the reputation of being a gathering for both classes'.

Behaviour was generally good and the Chief Superintendent of the Borough Police reported in 1860 that the races had been 'as quiet as a Methodist meeting'. Apart from a few outspoken critics among the Dissenting ministers, there seems to have been no antipathy to the races. Attendances were rising and a new stand was built in 1866. But in July 1883 the sport was re-located to the track at Oadby, two miles out of town. The decision was entirely due to the preference of the Jockey Club who now charged gate money and who did not want competition from the old established annual event. (Jeremy Crump, *The Great Carnival of the Year: the Leicester Races in the 19th Century*, T.L.A.S. LVIII 1982-3.)

For many years afterwards local people still referred to the park as the 'Race Course'. Calling such a bare expanse of grass a 'park' was originally a joke. Ideas of what constitutes a park change, but to contemporaries the ideal was something carefully designed to please the eye, with flower beds, exotic shrubs, water features and preferably a grotto—precisely what was to be found in Abbey Park which opened in 1882.

Leicester was, in fact, the very first town council to set aside land for the recreation of its citizens in the Welford Road Recreation Ground, in 1839. It was re-named Nelson Mandela Park in honour of the great South African statesman. As the town grew in the later 19th century, so its citizens felt the need for places of recreation, especially in the lower and poorer districts along the Belgrave Road. At the same time the River Soar to the west of this area was prone to flood and wound its way through water-logged land that Victorian opinion regarded as a breeding ground for malaria.

The editor of the *Leicester Chronicle*, James Thompson, took up the idea of one of his correspondents in calling for the creation of a people's park, to be fashioned out of a comprehensive draining of the area. In the middle he proposed 'a large pool or lakelet', while the soil excavated might be used 'to throw up earthen mounds and banks to diversify the surrounding surface with great success, and large masses of rock could be brought from no great distance to impart rustic boldness and fine effect to the landscape gardener's conception'. Thompson further proposed a cricket enclosure, a gymnasium and an aviary while a skating rink could be made on the pool in winter. All this, he said, could be realised within the 80 or 90 acres of the Abbey Meadow 'surrounded as it is with water channels'. Five years later, Thompson's dream was realised in the opening of Abbey Park by the Prince and Princess of Wales on Whit Monday, 29 May 1882. (See chapter on royal events page 102.)

Such municipal extravagance horrified Robert Read, the prudent author of a guide to Leicester, published the previous year. He denounced the idea of a park as 'our Corporation folly' and declared that 'the very large expenditure going on and contemplated in that dank, diphtherial and febrile spot' positively gave him 'the shivers'.

The pasture was also the scene of naked bathing for men. Women were expected to cover themselves in voluminous costumes, but men had always been accustomed to enjoy the freedom of skinny-dipping. 'The disgusting scenes tolerated in the pasture' were condemned by sober citizens like the town Missionary, Joseph Dare, but Sergeant Wright, the Inspector of Nuisances, saw nothing to cause offence, however, and the practice continued till well into the next century.

Cricket, too, was played on St Margaret's pasture, but in 1825 a permanent ground was acquired in Wharf Street with an adjacent bowling green. Wharf Street saw many famed cricket events. In one North v. South game before the advent of pads, the legendary Alfred Mynn suffered such serious injury from fast bowlers that he was unable to play again for two years. The matches that excited most enthusiasm were those played between an All-England team of eleven men against a local side of twenty-two. The England team usually won, but in 1856 and again in 1860 victory went to Leicestershire. The second occasion was the last game to be played on the Wharf Street ground, as it was sold and built upon in the same year.

Thereafter cricket matches were played on the race course but, in 1878, Grace Road was opened. At the time, this was still beyond the town limits and so, in 1895, when the club became a first-class county, ground was bought on Aylestone Road closer to the city. Major fixtures still took place at Grace Road, however, and in the 1970s it was bought by the club as its permanent home.

The Leicestershire Club frequently proved its metal; in 1888 it defeated a touring Australian team and the early years of the 20th century were known as its Golden Age. In 1906 the opening batsmen knocked up 380 for the first wicket against Worcestershire. On another occasion, the opening batsman, C.J.B.Wood, carried his bat through both innings against Yorkshire, getting a hundred in each.

The club had its moments of glory in the first half of the 20th century, as when in 1929 George Geary took all ten wickets against Glamorgan for 18 runs, at Pontypridd. In 1955, C.H. Palmer took eight wickets for seven runs against Surrey. In fact he took them for not a single run. It was only in the following two overs that the seven runs were scored. Incredible as it may seem, the doctor had, earlier in the season, advised him not to bowl!

But it was not till the arrival of Ray Illingworth in 1969 that the fortunes of the county really began to improve dramatically. He led Leicestershire to victory in the Benson and Hedges Cup in 1972 and 1975 and, in the latter year, it won the County Championship for the first time. 1975 was also the year in which Leicestershire defeated the Australian touring team and in which David Gower became captain. Gower brought his own lustre and elegance to the county team, which he continued to lead until 1989.

Leicester Fosse Football Club began life as part of a men's group attached to a local church. It was formed in 1884, by members of the Emanuel Baptist Bible Class together with Old Wyggestonians, ex-pupils of the Wyggeston Boys school. In 1891, they moved to grounds in Filbert Street and, in the same year, gained entry to the Midland League. The Fosse retained its name till 1919 when it became Leicester City Football Club. Not always in the front rank, it was briefly in the first division in 1908 but sank back into obscurity for much of the 20th century. Its fortunes changed in the 1960s, since when it has produced a series of outstanding players, including the brilliant goal-keepers Gordon Banks and Peter Shilton, and the strikers Gary Linneker and Emile Heskey.

In contrast to the chequered history of the City at Filbert Street, Leicester has always excelled at rugby. Three clubs joined together in 1880 to form Leicester Football Club and, in 1891, 'the Tigers', nicknamed after the county regiment, moved from grounds on Belgrave Road to Welford Road. It soon became recognised as one of the best in England. *The Times* once declared it the best ground after Twickenham.

1977-8 saw the Tigers reach the final of the John Player Cup, a title they won for the next three seasons. Twenty years later, Leicestershire had

38 *Sporting Triumph, the statue commemorating a year in which Leicester achieved success in three major sporting events.*

39 *The old hall at Kirkby Mallory before it was demolished and the grounds turned into a race track.*

spectacular success in three major sporting events. The County Cricket Club held the county championship in 1996, Leicester City Football Club won the Coca-Cola Cup in their first season after promotion to the Premier League (1996-7), and the Tigers won the Pilkington Cup (1996-97). As a result, Tony Banks, the Sports Minister, dubbed Leicester the nation's 'Sporting Capital', and a popular campaign was launched to honour the county's sporting heroes with a permanent memorial.

Kirkby Mallory, now the home of motor-cycle events, was formerly the ancestral seat of the Noel family. Anne Isabella Milbanke, heiress to the Noel family, married the poet Byron in 1816 but separated from him within a year of her daughter's birth. Ada Lovelace, the daughter, was the confidant and lover of Thomas Babbage, the mathematician and inventor of a proto-type computer. She was kept, as far as possible, away from any knowledge of her father, the poet, and never allowed to read his poems or even to see his portrait. Unsurprisingly, she developed into a somewhat eccentric individual. She was fascinated by the idea of flying—'flyology' as

WYGGESTON GRAMMAR SCHOOL FOR BOYS, LEICESTER
IN THE GREAT HALL, ON DECEMBER 16th and 17th, at 7-30 p.m.

The Wyggeston Dramatic Society presents

"H.M.S. PINAFORE"
Or "THE LASS THAT LOVED A SAILOR"

WRITTEN BY **W. S. GILBERT**   (By permission of R. D'Oyly Carte, Esq.)   COMPOSED BY ARTHUR SULLIVAN

DRAMATIS PERSONÆ

The Rt. Hon Sir Joseph Porter, K.C.B. (First Lord of the Admiralty)	H. Dexter	
Captain Corcoran (Commanding H.M.S. Pinafore)	P. H. J. Browett	
Ralph Rackstraw (Able Seaman)	B. W. Eyre	
Dick Deadeye (Able Seaman)	A. W. Gayton	
Bill Bobstay (Bosun's Mate)	D. F. Biddles	
Bob Beckett (Carpenter's Mate)	R. F. Martin	
Josephine (The Captain's Daughter)	R. A. Gowing	
Hebe (Sir Joseph's First Cousin)	G. T. Hadfield	
Little Buttercup (a Portsmouth Bumboat Woman)	P. D. Russell	
Middie	J. M. Attenborough	

FIRST LORD'S SISTERS, COUSINS AND AUNTS

J. E. Adderson   D. G. W. Cox   D. Snashall
P. J. Allen   C. J. Curtis   M. C. B. Stilwell
N. H. Allison   R. P. Davies   R. M. Thompson
R. K. Ashlin   J. R. Downes   J. L. W. Towler
D. F. Attenborough   M. E. Johnson   J. L. Waterfield
J. S. Bradshaw   A. T. B. Jones   R. G. W. Wheatley
H. C. Briten   W. R. Parkins   J. L. Yearley
G. R. Burnham   C. D. M. Playfair   P. A. Young

SAILORS, MARINES, etc.

R. S. Attenborough   A. R. Charlesworth   J. M. Hubbard
D. Bacon   C. J. D. Chegwyn   J. G. Roberts
E. B. Bish   L. W. Clarke   J. M. Rowland
P. A. Bramley   C. G. D. Dennis   R. J. Symes
P. G. Burgess   D. W. F. Folley   R. T. Wright
H. P. Carpenter

SCENE
Quarterdeck of H.M.S. Pinafore (off Portsmouth)   Act I.—Noon   Act II.—Night

There will be one interval of 15 minutes during which coffee will be served in the Dining Hall

THE ORCHESTRA (COMPOSED OF PAST AND PRESENT WYGGESTONIANS)

1st Violin — Mr. J. R. Scott, Mr. E. N. Sharpe, N. F. Moore
2nd Violin — Mr. Leeson, P. F. Ward, P. S. Welch, A. W. Howe, C. H. Gilbert
Viola — Mr. F. J. Marlow
Cello — Mr. H. F. Hopkins, Mr. D. J. Crabb
D. Bass — Mr. W. Warden
Flute — Mr. L. W. Cullen, Mr. W. G. Barton
Oboe — Mr. A. Thornley
Clarinet — Mr. F. Allt
Cornet — Mr. E. Moore
Trombone — Mr. S. Blastock, W. J. Herbert
Drums — Mr. D. V. Cooke
Pianoforte

LEADER   ROBERT SILVESTER, L.R.A.M.   CONDUCTOR   D. BYRON-SCOTT

40 *Programme for* HMS Pinafore, *performed by the Wyggeston Boys School in 1934, with all three Attenborough boys in the cast list.*

41 *The Princess and Sir Richard Attenborough at the Opening of the Richard Attenborough Centre for Disability and the Arts, 1995.*

42 *Elephants being taken to Bertram Mills' Circus at Melton Mowbray in 1935.*

43 *(right) The May Fair at Castle Donington.*

she called it. Her grasp of scientific theory was so acute that she devoted all her energy to encouraging Babbage's experiments with his Analytical machine or computer. Her book on the subject became a sensation, and the first American computer software language was christened 'Ada' in her honour.

In 1919, the University College of Leicester was established in the former Leicestershire and Rutland Lunatic Asylum, under the guidance of Rattray. The second man to hold this office was F. L. Attenborough. He lived with his family in College House, originally built for John Buck, Superintendent of the Asylum and, prior to that, the town's first Medical Officer of Health. The Attenborough family, including David and Richard, were consequently brought up in College House, later moving to Knighton Hall, now the official residence of the Vice-Chancellor of Leicester University.

LEICESTERSHIRE AT LEISURE / 47

Sir Richard Attenborough's interest in the arts led him to sponsor a purpose-built centre for Disability and the Arts, which was opened by Diana Princess of Wales in 1995.

Public concern for the welfare of animals and legislation controlling performing animals has virtually brought about the demise of a once popular family entertainment. A sight never likely to be seen again is this photograph taken at Melton Mowbray of three elephants taking part in Bertram Mills' travelling circus in 1935.

In the county villages, church fêtes and garden parties still provide the focus of much communal activity and enjoyment, but the celebration of May Day is almost a thing of the past. That it continues to give rise to annual festivities is clear from the photograph of children dancing round the maypole in Castle Donington.

Six
IN TIME OF WAR

Early Victorian England was not free from violence or the fear of class conflict. The French Revolution, and the two decades of war with France which ended in 1815 with the battle of Waterloo, were still close enough in time to strike fear into the hearts of the propertied classes, whenever there was talk of political reform. The Chartists, who argued for manhood suffrage and other perfectly reasonable demands, were seen by many as dangerous radicals intent on securing by force what could not be obtained by peaceful means.

In Leicester, Thomas Cooper pushed aside more cautious leaders of the movement and established his own ascendancy over the local Chartists. Fired by his words, some hundreds of working men gathered in Humberstone Gate one summer evening in 1842 with the intention of marching to Belgrave. What they would then have done is not clear, but there occurred instead what used to be called in school history books the 'Battle of Mowmacre Hill'.

It was in no way a threat to society, and the men were quickly dispersed. The local paper reported the incident in the following words: 'A meeting of about 1500 men and women was held this morning in Humberstone Gate ... Several speakers addressed the assemblage in a very violent strain; the purport of which was that if the military showed their bayonets they (the people) would show them stones and sticks. At seven o'clock a body of police under Mr Goodyer, proceeded to

44 *Mafeking celebrations in Market Harborough.*

49

45 *Men of E Company of the 5th Territorial Battalion of the Leicestershire Regiment parade on The Square, Market Harborough, prior to marching to Loughborough, 6 August 1914.*

46 *Signing-up for service in the Great War at the Magazine in Leicester. Most of these men would not return, but those who did received a hero's welcome.*

47 *Peace celebrations, Shepshed, 1919.*

Belgrave in a coach and four. Upon dismounting and making towards the place of meeting, the mob at once dispersed, running in every direction over hedge and ditch.'

It was a farce and a fiasco rather than a battle. The only casualty seems to have been a water-pump shot at during a night patrol of the streets. It is said that long after the event, if one of the Yeoman Cavalry walked through the town in uniform, he was likely to be pursued by the inquiry: 'Who shot the pump?' As for Thomas Cooper, he spent some months in Stafford gaol and devoted his later life to working men's education and to writing his memoirs.

The first war to shake confidence in the invincibility of the British army was the South African campaign of 1898 to 1902. Not only was this

48 *Children of Servicemen being entertained at the Picture House in Loughborough in December 1914.*

a conflict that divided the nation as to its moral justification; for many it was an instance of colonial oppression against a brave people struggling to be free, but it was also a contest in which the British Tommy was no match for guerrilla fighters, sure of their own ground and familiar with the local terrain.

A series of harrowing defeats made the relief of one besieged township the signal for unprecedented national euphoria. Mafeking found its way into

IN TIME OF WAR / 53

national folklore as a great victory just as Dunkirk did four decades later.

When the Great War broke out in 1914 there was widespread confidence that it would all be over by Christmas, and young men flocked to the colours, anticipating excitement and glory rather than the abject misery of trench warfare. If nothing else, the war brought an end to unemployment.

Few families escaped the agony of the First World War as a generation of young men left their homeland, but it was only they who felt the raw

49 *Damage caused by a Zeppelin raid on Loughborough in 1916 which resulted in the deaths of four men and six women.*

54 / LEICESTERSHIRE EVENTS

50 & 51 *Here we see children collecting aluminium and boys filling sand bags, used to protect buildings from the effects of bomb blast.*

reality of death and physical suffering. At home it was possible to read censored accounts of battles and to take comfort that it was all a long way off. But this cannot be said of the Second World War, when aerial bombardment brought the carnage and uncertainty of war into the homes of ordinary citizens. But if there was carnage, there was also cameraderie and the feeling that everyone could do his bit in the war effort.

Coventry is well-known for the hammering it took in 1940, but Leicester, too, had its share of air raids. During the same night that saw the destruction of Coventry, bombs fell over many parts of Leicestershire. Cavendish Road off Aylestone Road in Leicester seems to have been hit on account of its proximity to the gas works which mercifully escaped by a few yards. Also hit that night were Essex Road and Highfield Street, where 52 people lost their lives.

/ 55

52 *Evacuees coming to Loughborough to escape from the Blitz.*

The Town Hall in Leicester received a direct hit, but fortunately the bomb failed to explode and was eventually recovered from the cellar. Less fortunate was the pavilion on Victoria Park. Another well-known target which was utterly destroyed was the works of Freeman Hardy and Willis on the corner of Rutland Street and Humberstone Road.

When the war ended in 1945, a wave of relief swept over the country as life returned to something like normality. There were street parties everywhere, and the camaraderie of wartime transformed momentarily into the euphoria of peace.

53 *Remembrance Day at Castle Hill, Mountsorrel, 1992.*

Seven
CRIME AND PUNISHMENT

As crime is defined by society, and as society is constantly changing, making the punishment fit the crime is one of those tasks that can never be regarded as finished. What was once regarded as a capital offence, such as stealing a pocket-handkerchief, no longer rates so severe a penalty. Other crimes no longer exist, like sex between consenting adults. Witchcraft is another crime that, happily, no longer invites the attention of the law, but, early in the 17th century, it was deemed to be rife, and many an old woman was harried and tormented after being branded as a witch.

In 1616, nine women were hanged for supposedly bewitching a 12-year-old boy from Husband's Bosworth. He was evidently prone to fits during which he made sounds like those of various animals, which were diagnosed as familiar spirits of the nine women.

The following year, three women from Belvoir suffered the death penalty for supposedly causing the death of the son of the Earl of Rutland. Joan Flower and her daughters, Margaret and Philippa, were employed at the castle as cleaners. They were, apparently, an unpleasant trio who swore and cursed at their neighbours and never went to church. Margaret was caught pilfering from the castle and lost her job, though she was given 40 shillings and other gifts on leaving. The three women were accused of plotting revenge on the earl and his family by casting spells on them.

Be that as it may, in 1613 Henry, the son of the earl, sickened and died of an unknown illness. According to their prosecutors, the women then turned their attention to Francis, the second son and his sister, Katherine. Rumours of their witchcraft reached the ears of the earl and his wife, and the three women were arrested in 1617, together with three more from other villages in the county.

The women were all taken for trial at Lincoln, where Joan protested her innocence, calling for bread and water, and saying that if she were guilty it would choke her. Sure enough, on eating a piece of bread, she immediately died. The shock of this sudden bereavement led her two terrified daughters to describe in graphic detail all their evil deeds. Confession may have

54 *The interior of Bottesford church with the Manners monuments.*

brought solace but it did not procure freedom and they were hanged for murder in March 1618.

In a less credulous age we are inclined to dismiss all talk of witchcraft and to see the Flower family as innocent victims of superstitious nonsense. The earl, however, clearly believed they had engineered the death of his sons for there is, in Bottesford church, a monument to Francis, the 6th Earl, which records that: 'He Had Two Sons Both Wch Died In Their Infancy By Wicked Practice and Sorcerye.'

Belief in witches and their powers continued late into the 18th century. As late as 1760, two old women from Great Glen challenged each other as witches and agreed to be tried by the ordeal of swimming. They were accordingly stripped to their shifts, their thumbs and toes tied together and then thrown into a pool with a cart rope about their middle. One sank immediately thus proving her innocence but the other struggled on the surface—an infallible sign of guilt. She was pulled out and made to impeach her accomplices. At this she told of an old woman living in Burton Overy, who, she said, was 'as much witches as she was'.

Happily for the old dame from Great Glen, this was enough to divert attention to the poor creature from Burton. She, not surprisingly, locked herself in an upstairs room but the mob broke down the door and took her off to a gravel pit where her thumbs and toes were tied in the approved fashion before she was thrown into the water. Though the process was repeated several times she did not die and was left to recover on the bank. The perpetrators of this brutality were sentenced to the pillory and imprisoned for a month.

In the same year, the death of a land agent at the hands of Earl Ferrers led to one of the most celebrated trials in history. The earl was not known for his even temper and, having made up his mind that his land agent was siding with his estranged wife in a matrimonial dispute, took the rather extreme step of inviting the steward to his drawing room and killing him.

It was clearly a pre-meditated act, for the earl had sent most of the male servants out of the house and told his mistress to go to her father's house some two miles away, taking their children with her. When John Johnson, the unfortunate steward, came into the room he was accused of all manner of misdeeds and promptly told to kneel on the floor. Ferrers then shot him. Remorse apparently overcame the earl, and the doctor was summoned. Johnson was put to bed but it was too late to save him and he died the next day. The earl was arrested and taken to Ashby and then to Leicester gaol. A fortnight later he was taken to the Tower of London. Tried at Westminster Hall, he pleaded insanity but was found guilty and sentenced to hang at Tyburn—the first peer to suffer death by hanging from a scaffold.

At the other end of the social scale, workers in domestic industries were becoming alarmed at the growth of power-machinery that threatened to take away their jobs. Machine smashing was not unknown before the industrial revolution, but it took on a new significance as more and more employers sought to introduce labour-saving devices. Such resort to physical violence against machines was widespread in industrial areas, and Leicestershire weavers took such 'direct action' in the riots of 1773 and 1787.

A number of attempts were made to change production methods in the hosiery trade by introducing improved stocking frames. In 1773, two Leicester hosiers attempted to utilise an improved and simplified frame that was said to produce cheaper goods. Feelings among the operatives ran so high that a demonstration model of the new machine was paraded round the town and deliberately pulled to pieces. Such was the suspicion and hostility toward it, that the hosiers agreed not to introduce any new frame that might reduce employment in the industry.

Fourteen years later an attempt was made to bring new technology to bear on the production of worsted yarn. John Coltman, Joseph Whetstone and Joseph Brookhouse formed a partnership, in 1787, to make worsted yarn using the roller-spinning technique developed by Sir Richard Arkwright for spinning cotton yarn. Despite efforts to placate the workers, an angry crowd gathered outside the homes of Coltman and Whetstone, smashing their windows and looting a warehouse. Whetstone attempted to stop the destruction of his property by firing into the mob, which probably did little to cool tempers and led to at least one serious injury.

Coltman and Whetstone left town for a fortnight, but Brookhouse was singled out for special abuse as the inventor of the machine. He was burned in effigy and obliged to leave Leicester for good. The rioters pursued him to Market Harborough where they broke into his house and burned the prototype of the offending machine. Two days later a crowd of workers marched on Melton Mowbray where they had heard of another labour-threatening machine. This time they were met at the bridge outside Melton by a party of soldiers, but the machine was handed over to them voluntarily and destroyed.

What is most remarkable in these riots is the behaviour of the authorities. They appear to have had more sympathy with the rioting workers than with the beleaguered entrepreneurs. This perverse attitude resulted from political and religious hostility to the employers, who were all members of the Independent chapel in Bond Street, soon to be known as the Unitarian Great Meeting. These radical businessmen were solidly opposed to the Tory Corporation.

Thus, when a public notice appeared in the local paper inviting opponents of the new machinery to assemble the following week at a stated time and place, nothing was done to prevent this happening. When the riots began, the Mayor, who had been asked to intervene, did so only after the attackers had pilfered houses and destroyed property. He apparently told the crowd, 'Good boys, you have done enough, you had better give over and go home!' The next night while he was trying to read the Riot Act, someone threw a stone which injured him. He never fully recovered and died some months later.

John Coltman's son records in his memoirs that the magistrates refused to provide any protection until the partners promised not to conduct any worsted spinning by machinery within 50 miles of Leicester. As a result, the new techniques in spinning yarn developed elsewhere, and Leicester manufacturers had to send for yarn to make up for the deficiencies of local supply. Joseph Whetstone sued the Corporation for its incompetence in suppressing the riots and eventually won £250 in compensation. Clearly the riots of 1787 were not simply acts of mindless vandalism against machinery. A full account of this episode is given by Dr David Wykes in the *Transactions of the Leicestershire Archaeological and Historical Society*, 1987.

It was a disgruntled Leicestershire stocking-maker, Ned Ludd, who gave machine-smashing its familiar name, 'Luddism', in about 1811. Ned is said to have objected to being told to 'square his needles' and, according to the Nottingham historian, John Blackner, he took a hammer and proceeded to beat his father's stocking frames into a heap. Attacks on stocking frames were frequent in Nottingham and in Hinckley in the next few years, as a protest against wage reductions, but Leicestershire as a whole was much less affected by these Luddite riots because of the relative prosperity of its trade. This prosperity resulted from an invention known as 'Dawson's wheels' which made possible the manufacture of decorated, quality stockings. It was a short-lived boom because, with the change in fashion to clothes that covered the ankles, decorative fancy hosiery was no longer in such demand. But it so happened that the fashion for patterned hose just coincided with the classic period of Luddism and made Leicester workers less inclined to destroy the means of their own livelihood.

The most celebrated instance of Luddite activity in Leicestershire was the attack upon John Heathcoat's lace factory in Loughborough. Heathcoat had developed an entirely new method of producing lace on a variant of the stocking-frame. It was far cheaper than the traditional hand-made lace, and Heathcoat had great difficulty in keeping the secret of his machine from the prying eyes of competitors. He had already taken a lease on a property in Devon, when the attack on his Loughborough factory took place in June 1816.

A gang of 16 men led by James Towle entered the works, forced the employees to the ground and proceeded to smash 53 frames. It was the last straw for Heathcoat and he moved his entire operations to Tiverton in Devon, where the firm still exists today. Towle was eventually brought to justice and hanged. He refused to name his accomplices but, some months later, six of them were betrayed by an informer, and eventually hanged outside Leicester gaol. A newspaper account described them as 'fine looking young men, in the prime of life, health and vigour'. Fifteen thousand watched their execution and many joined them in singing hymns as they awaited their fate.

Belief in the deterrent power of the death penalty waned somewhat in the early 19th century, and juries often refused to impose the due penalty for trivial offences, such as stealing a loaf of bread. Reforming Home Secretaries cut the number of capital offences and introduced a modern system of policing that effectively reduced the amount of petty crime.

Serious misdeeds were, of course, dealt with severely and it was still assumed that public execution and display of the criminal's corpse would have a sobering effect on the populace at large. So, in 1832, when James Cook was found guilty of murder he was not only hanged but put up on public display in an iron basket.

Cook was a bookbinder in Wellington Street and he evidently found himself with a cash-flow problem. His solution was to entice a business acquaintance from London into his shop and to clobber him over the head for the sake of the money in his pockets.

The murderer was quite cool and deliberate in his method of disposing of the remains of his victim, cutting him up and burning him in the oven behind his shop. A passing constable asked about the consequent smell and was told it came from some old bones he had bought for his dog. Cook then went home for the night, but the constable's suspicions were aroused and he returned to the scene to examine the ashes. A few charred finger bones were enough to convince him that Cook was up to no good.

James Cook was eventually captured as he attempted to board a ship leaving Liverpool for America. His corpse was hung near the junction of Welford Road and Aylestone Road not far from the county gaol. He was the last man to be gibbeted in England. The actual iron basket or gibbet now forms part of the national prison museum collection at Newbold Revill, near Rugby, but a replica hangs in the Guildhall at Leicester.

In 1836 the county town was quick to follow the example of London in establishing a modern police force. It even brought in several officers from the Metropolitan force, including the first Head Constable. The work of the new bobbies was at first regarded with suspicion by some citizens. The *Leicester Journal* declaimed against this step on the road to 'continental despotism', but opinion soon swung in favour of the new force, as petty crime went down and the criminal fraternity moved to fresh pastures.

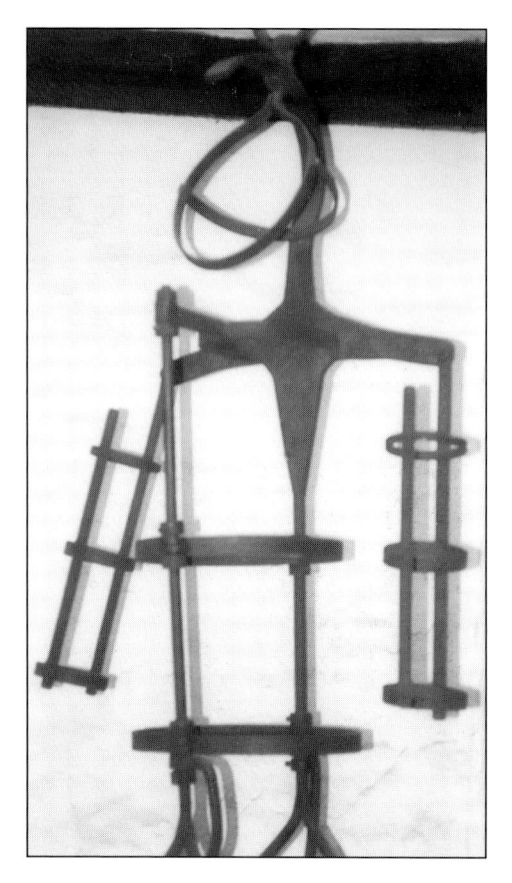

55 *Gibbet in the Guildhall, a replica of that in which the body of James Cook was hung.*

A success story of detection in Victorian Leicestershire concerned the disappearance of the heir to the Winstanley estates in Braunstone. Winstanley had taken himself to the continent in June 1862, and his family lost all contact with him. As the weeks passed, their concern grew, and a reward of ten pounds was offered for anyone solving the mystery.

Winstanley had just been appointed High Sheriff of Leicestershire and had agreed to be present at an investiture meeting, and he had also agreed to take part in an Archaeological Congress soon to take place in Leicester. Francis 'Tanky' Smith, a detective with the Leicester force, went to work on the case, tracing Winstanley's movements from Folkestone to Calais, Cologne and, finally, Coblenz. There, at about midnight on 7 June, he had been crossing the Moselle in a ferry boat when he fell into the water and was drowned.

The body was found five days later and buried as that of a person unknown. 'Tanky' Smith had it exhumed and identified as that of the missing Winstanley.

Quite what caused Winstanley to disappear is not clear. The newspaper accounts hint at foul play in that two ten-pound notes, obtained by the deceased in London, were presented at the Bank, some time after his disappearance, by a German. It was rumoured that Winstanley was a member of a secret continental society and had been kidnapped for violating its rules. The newspapers described him as a 'high private character' and spoke of his 'habitual reserve and peculiarity of action'. After listing his virtues and noting his gift of new schools to the children of Kirby Muxloe, the writer described him as 'retiring and unostentatious' and remarked that 'Mr Winstanley had not made the figure in the county which his birth, estate and name would warrant; but an expectation was beginning to be entertained that he would shortly fulfil the best hopes of his family connections and friends.'

Reading between the lines, it would seem likely that the newly appointed High Sheriff was not a very stable character and that he may well have taken his own life. He had apparently gone to some trouble to make the identification of his body difficult, possibly cutting out the initials on his clothing. Perhaps the thought of being pushed into the limelight was more than he could cope with, or he may have genuinely intended to disappear and accidentally fell out of the ferry boat.

The story is often rehearsed because of the skill displayed by 'Tanky' Smith. He is said to have received a large reward from the grateful, if grieving, relatives. This must have been much above the original offer of ten pounds, for it enabled him to retire from the force and make a good deal of money in land and property deals. His name is perpetuated in Francis Street, off Stoneygate Road, and his face appears, adorned in a variety of disguises he is said to have assumed in his work as a detective, on the facade of Top Hat Terrace, the block of houses opposite Saxby Street on London Road in Leicester, which was designed by his architect son.

If James Cook's was the most notorious murder trial of the

56 *A newspaper illustration of the last days of James Cook, 1832.*

57 *'Tanky' Smith in one of his disguises on the façade of Top Hat Terrace on London Road.*

19th century in Leicestershire, then the Green Bicycle mystery must surely be the most celebrated trial of the 20th century. Interest in the death of Bella Wright engaged the press and public for some weeks after her body was found, and attention was focused on the identity of a man, seen with Bella on the evening of her death, riding a green bicycle.

The case would have ceased to be newsworthy and become one of those unsolved mysteries, gathering dust in police files, had it not been for a series of chance happenings some months later. The first incident occurred, in 1919, when a barge-owner was pulling on a rope by the canal bank near St Mary's Mill. As the rope surfaced he saw the frame of a green bicycle emerge from the water. The cycle was examined by the police and was found to bear a number which ultimately established the identity of the owner.

The machine had been bought by Ronald Light from a Derby cycle dealer in 1910. When Light was confronted with the facts, he first denied ever having had a bicycle but later admitted it was his. He claimed to have disposed of the machine for fear of being incriminated, in view of the

58 *Ronald Light, accused of the murder.*

59 *The scene of the crime, on the Gartree road, near Little Stretton.*

publicity given to the hunt for a green bicycle. The circumstantial evidence was quite enough to bring him to trial for murder.

60 *The bicycle hauled from the canal.*

Ronald Light was a liar and a philanderer who had twice cheated his way out of active service in France. But to the public he was an ex-serviceman reputedly suffering from shell-shock, for whom every allowance should be made. Marshall Hall, the most brilliant defence lawyer of the day, managed to convince the jury that Light was innocent. He left Leicestershire after the trial and lived on the Isle of Sheppey, dying aged 90 in Sittingbourne, Kent, in 1975.

Several events in more recent criminal history have close connections with Leicestershire. It was at the University of Leicester that Sir Alex Jeffries made his historic breakthrough with the discovery of DNA finger-printing, establishing the existence of genetic coding in DNA material that would prove a unique identification for every human being. It was also here in

Leicestershire that one of the first convictions for murder came about through the evidence of DNA testing.

Two girls were murdered on footpaths in the Narborough area, just south of Leicester. They had both been raped and strangled. The police arrested a man who actually confessed to the murder of one of the girls but not to the other. Sir Alex was called in to determine whether both had been assaulted by the same man. Tests confirmed that one man was indeed responsible but that neither murder had been committed by the youth in custody.

Determined to catch the real culprit, the police began, in January 1987, an exhaustive testing of every man in the neighbourhood of Narborough, Enderby and Littlethorpe. Altogether nearly 4,000 samples were taken, but none corresponded with the traces found on the victims. The case looked as if it would end as another unsolved mystery. Then one evening in the following August, a conversation overheard in *The Clarendon* public house, in Leicester, led to further progress. The conversation concerned a man called Colin Pitchfork, who had persuaded a colleague to take the DNA test on his behalf. Pitchfork told his friend that he had earlier taken the test for a man who was scared of needles and that, when he was invited to take the test himself, he was afraid that his 'good deed' would get him into trouble.

61 *Sir Alex Jeffries receiving the Freedom of the City outside the Town Hall in Leicester.*

Pitchfork was arrested and admitted to both murders, giving detailed accounts of how he went about them. On the first occasion he had dropped his wife at an evening class, leaving his son in the child seat of the car while he went to look for a victim. After the second murder he had returned home and baked a cake!

The man who was foolish enough to provide a sample for the murderer was given a suspended sentence of 18 months. Pitchfork himself was given two life sentences and two ten-year sentences for rape. Alex Jeffries received the Freedom of the City of Leicester, a well-deserved knighthood and a chair at Leicester University.

Eight
TRANSPORTATION

Roads

Few counties have a more eventful history of transportation than Leicestershire. It is traversed by the ancient Fosse Way that runs through England from the south coast in Dorset to Lincoln and beyond. When the Romans came they devised their own metalled version of the Fosse and laid further roads to Colchester, the via Devana, and to Mancetter on the road known as Watling Street, that eventually took travellers across Anglesey to Ireland.

The network of roads established by the Romans fell into disrepair in the centuries after they left Britain, but the roads never fell into complete decay. They were always essential to the process of distribution and marketing of goods and services and, as the economy grew in the 17th and 18th centuries, it became clear that something other than the age-old methods of repair were needed to keep them serviceable.

The solution, in times when opinion was even more hostile to taxation than it is today, lay in private initiative by public-spirited individuals who banded together in order to form trusts. These trusts undertook to repair and improve sections of the highway and charged folk for the privilege of using the roads under their care. Gates or bars were erected at each end of sections of highway so covered.

The Loughborough to Harborough turnpike set up in 1726 charged a shilling for a wagon with four horses clearing the entire road, a quarter of this being collected at each of the four gates. Pedestrians paid nothing, but horses and mules had to pay a penny at each gate and sheep and oxen five or ten pence per score.

Daniel Defoe was a great advocate of the turnpikes. He came to Leicester during his tour in the 1720s and castigated the unimproved road as 'perfectly frightful to travellers'. How far he would have seen a change for the better after the establishment of the Harborough turnpike is open to question. Every journey by coach would be an event to the inexperienced traveller, and encountering the Leicester turnpike to Market Harborough was no exception. A traveller from the continent in 1782 recounted his experiences as a passenger on the stage coach from Leicester. He was keen to travel

62 *The Tollgate on Thorpe Road, Loughborough.*

63 *The final days of one of Leicester's most famous coaching inns is celebrated here. It shows the last stage coach leaving the* Three Crowns Hotel *in 1866. The inn took its name from the union of the three kingdoms of England, Scotland and Hanover in 1714. It was demolished to make way for the present Natwest Bank on the corner of Granby Street and Horsefair Street in 1867.*

and not being able to obtain a seat inside the coach took his chance on the top but he was so uncomfortable there that, ignoring the advice of a fellow passenger, he decided to crawl into the basket with the luggage:

> As long as we went uphill [he wrote] it was easy and pleasant ... but how was the case altered when we came to go downhill; then all the trunks and parcels began, as it were, to dance around me and everything in the basket seemed to be alive; and I every moment received from them such violent blows, that I thought my last hour was come ... I was obliged to suffer this torture nearly an hour, till we came to another hill again, when quite shaken to pieces and sadly bruised, I again crept to the top of the coach, and took possession of my former seat.

It was, he wrote, 'a warning to all strangers to stage coaches who may happen to take it into their heads, without being used to it, to take a place on the outside of an English postcoach; and still more, a place in the basket'.

Canals

Turnpike roads enabled men and women to travel much faster especially after the development of macadamised road surfaces, but the transport of heavy goods, such as coal, stone and timber, required new thinking if it were to expand. One of the first to recognise the need for improved water transport was a Northamptonshire landowner, Sir Thomas Skipwith of Newbold Revill. In 1634 he set about building a canal from the river Trent to Loughborough. He ran out of money and the scheme came to nothing but, had it succeeded, he would have entered the history books as the pioneer of canal transport over a century before the Duke of Bridgewater.

It was Bridgewater's success with his canal from Worsley to Manchester that set businessmen thinking along similar lines in the land-locked county of Leicestershire. James Brindley, the Duke's brilliant engineer, was called in to survey a line, but the project appeared too costly, and it was not till 1778 that the Soar Navigation was actually opened to Loughborough, bringing coal mined in the Nottingham and Derbyshire coalfield. The Soar Navigation became the most profitable in the entire country, its £100 shares selling for £4,600 a piece by 1824.

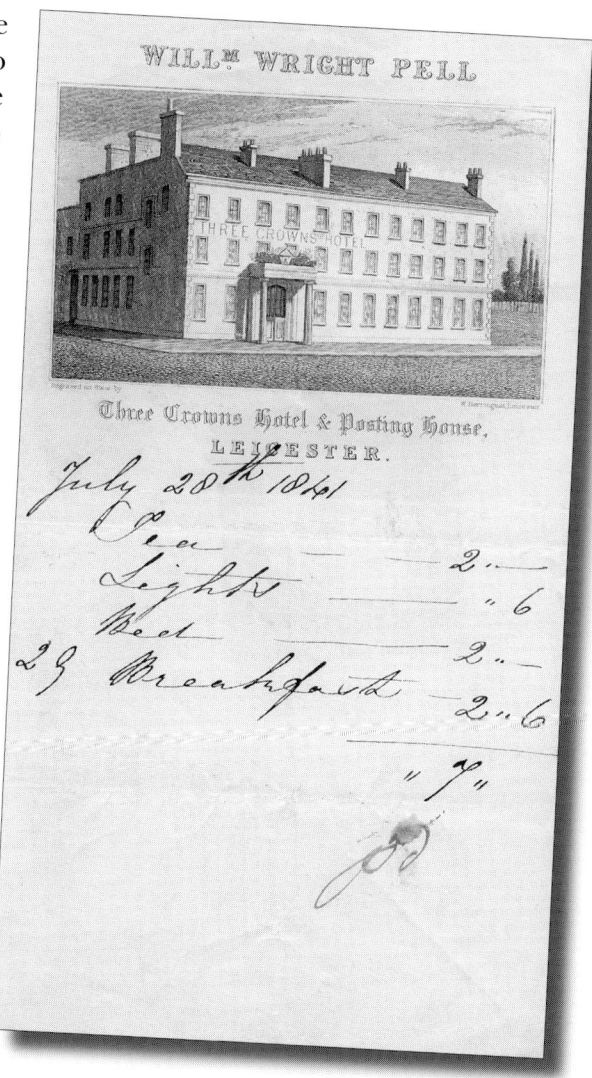

64 Copy of a bill for bed and breakfast at the Three Crowns in 1841.

65-6 *The Blackbrook Reservoir under construction, seen from above and below the dam, completed in 1906, as the source of Loughborough's water supply.*

It needed no genius to predict the ensuing clamour for an extension of the canal to Leicester. In addition to the benefits of cheap fuel in the county, there was the prospect of vast profits from potential through-traffic with London. But there was still the question of coal from West Leicestershire. With Nottingham and Derbyshire coal coming down from the Erewash valley, across the Trent and down the Soar Navigation to Loughborough, Leicestershire coal owners, with no access to water transport, found it hard to compete. They feared an extension to Leicester would seal their fate even more firmly, so for 16 years there was a stalemate, and no extension to the Soar Navigation.

The impasse was resolved by the making of a separate canal linking the collieries in the region of Swannington to Loughborough. Under this agreement, the Leicester Navigation would carry coal from both coalfields. Accordingly, in October 1794, two

Transportation / 71

boats landed their cargoes of coal at the new wharf in Leicester, one from the Derby and Nottinghamshire field and the other from west Leicestershire, via the newly constructed Charnwood Forest Canal. The pledge to the Leicestershire coal owners had been observed, and henceforth coal flooded in to the Leicester market. It was an event of the utmost importance to the town and county. There were celebrations, dinners, speeches and one prominent citizen, John Coltman, even composed a poem to mark the occasion. He sang the praises of the canal, listing the variety of goods which would come by water to the town:

>Though Leicester has in some obscurity lay,
>Behold a dawn appears of brighter day;
>The wished event at last has taken place
>And now a smile is seen on every face:
>A boat has smoothly sailed up the Soar,
>It's freight is coals, and cold is felt no more.

Coltman went on to relate, in the same excruciating verse, some of the articles that would now arrive in Leicester from other places:

>From distant quarries we shall have our stone
>To pave our streets and face the lofty dome.
>…
>The iron which in heavy bars is wrought
>By this conveyance too is hither brought;
>And pigs of lead which are so useful here
>We soon shall see arrive from Derbyshire.
>…
>And other boats we hope we soon shall fill,
>With lime from Grace Dieu, also from Cloud Hill;
>The Norfolk wheat by water we shall see,
>To make us bread to feed the family:
>And millstones too by which we grind our corn,
>By water now we see are hither borne;
>The Norway oak which comes across the sea,
>And logs of beautiful mahogany.
>…
>Good porter too already here we see
>From Simpson's Nottingham brewery.
>Another boat you'll see with flowing sail,
>And deeply laden with fine Burton ale.

In the absence of any contemporary sketch these ponderous couplets must suffice to record the event.

As a solution to the problems of West Leicestershire coal owners, however, the Charnwood canal was a total failure. The Company had hoped to employ a system of 'container traffic' by transporting fully-laden coal tubs from the railways at the pit heads onto barges on the canal, taking them off the boats at Nanpantan and then by a stretch of railway line down to the canal at Loughborough basin. Evidently, the technical difficulties were not overcome, and the contents of the railway trucks had, therefore, to be manually emptied from the tubs onto canal boats, and the process repeated three times before coal joined the main channel.

If this were not enough to spoil its chances, there occurred in February 1799, a disaster of epic dimensions. Brian Williams relates the circumstances thus:

> The winter of 1798-9 was a bad one with very heavy falls of snow and freezing rain. The great thaw began in February and the Charnwood hills began their massive discharge of water into the streams. The Blackbrook resevoir lay, as indeed it still does, in the valley head of one of the most important of these streams on the northern flank of Charnwood. The dammed valley quickly filled and the discharging overflow weir was incapable of coping. The pressure on the dam itself became intolerable and at 11 o'clock in the morning on February 20th, with a noise like a 'clap of thunder' it burst and the reservoir emptied in some eleven minutes, ... Wreaking horrifying damage.

Brian Williams gives the text of a letter from Mr Herrick of Beaumanor Hall to his sister, describing the event in graphic detail:

> We were all going to Garendon about one o'clock to take leave of the family who were going to town but when we got to Loughborough the town was in a consternation. Coaches, horse and all were stopped by a deluge of water. The Telegraph coach saw it coming and was obliged to gallop with the coach to save their lives. When we got to within a mile of Garendon it was like the sea which roared as if to be heard a mile away and swept all before it—cattle, sheep, houses, hedges, corn fields and large oak trees were torn up by their roots and thrown down and stacks of corn and hay.
>
> When we arrived at Garendon all was consternation expecting account every moment of the destruction of Dishley Mill and Shepshed Mill and it carried away the bridge at Garendon and came close to the park wall and a large stack of hay was carried over several fields and hedges and set it down in a lane and left it quite perfect—it extended to Thorpe town and covered the Derby Road for a mile and a half in length. We saw cheese, loaves of bread, furniture of all sorts, beds, tables, ridge tiles of houses, doors, window frames etc. all brought down in the torrent. People up to the neck in water saving sheep of which vast numbers are drowned and getting out furniture, boxes etc. Whole fields of turnips washed away, wheat fields the same, a more dreadful sight I have never beheld. ...
>
> This dreadful calamity was occasioned by the breaking down of the whole bank of the reservoir in the Forest—a large farmhouse, a Mr Chesters situated by the side of Blackbrook near the Ashby Turnpike road ... the man and all his children had only two minutes to make their escape, the water rose instantly above the ridge tiles at the top of the house, turned the house round and dashed it down and not a vestige remains, they could not save either their clothes or furniture, all their money, writings etc. lost ...
>
> My brother and I set off for Blackbrook about five o'clock that evening to see it. The whole reservoir was empty in about eleven minutes, all the fields were like sands of the sea shore, not a blade of grass to be seen or a vestige of the buildings, not one stone left upon another. We do not know the particulars of the damage done at other places but it is supposed that it will cost the Navigation Company many thousands of pounds. There were more than 500 people from all parts there today and the roads full of more people going to view the scene. 40 men were at

67 *A regatta on the canal at Market Harborough in 1909. The first was held four years earlier.*

work to make the Turnpike Road passable. The men that stood on the bank of the reservoir moved just a minute before it fell, it burst like a clap of thunder and flew nearly fifty feet in the air.

The canal ceased to be navigable in the early 19th century but the reservoir built to service it remained and presented a coveted source of additional water supply for the Leicester Waterworks. However, when Leicester made moves to acquire it in 1885, Loughborough Town Council cunningly purchased riparian rights from Mr De Lisle of Garendon and thereby secured its future use. They were in no hurry to spend money on it, however, and it was twenty years before the new Blackbrook dam was completed. Disaster almost struck again in 1958, when an earthquake fractured its foundations but, mercifully, an after-shock restored it to its original position.

Unlike the railways, canals were never a viable means of passenger transport. Three miles an hour along circuitous routes that followed the contours or made use of time-consuming pound-locks, was hardly appealing to travellers on business. But the waterways have become a valued resource for pleasure-cruising and several disused routes have been re-opened in recent years.

In the early 1900s Bigg's Boat House at Aylestone provided a great attraction. Courting couples strolled along the canal bank or drifted in punts and canoes with fairy lights twinkling in the dusk.

Railways

The problem of transporting coal from the pits in the region of west Leicestershire was finally solved by the laying of a railway. It was opened in 1832 to the West Bridge in Leicester and it was one of the earliest lines to be built.

The Leicester and Swannington owed its origin to William Stenson of Whitwick, but it was the involvement of John Ellis, a Quaker farmer of Beaumont Leys, that got the scheme off the ground. Ellis knew George Stephenson and persuaded him to send his son Robert to design the Leicester Swannington line. Some of the original features survive to this day, including the mile-long Glenfield tunnel, now bricked up at each end, and its ventilation shafts. The lift-bridge designed to take the line over the canal to the coal yard of John Ellis and Company was removed and re-erected at the Snibston Discovery Park, and the stationary engine, used to haul trucks up an incline at Swannington, is now on display at the Railway Museum at York.

68 *The Swannington inclined plane.*

Nine years after the opening of Leicester's first railway and one year after the coming of its second, the Midland Counties Railway, Thomas Cook hit upon the idea which was to bring him fame and fortune. He determined to hire a whole train for a temperance excursion to Loughborough. It was the beginning of the modern package tour industry. By the time he died in 1891, Cook had taken parties to India, Egypt and all quarters of the globe, supplying them with detailed advice and ensuring their comfort and convenience at all times.

Conflicting interests frequently delay progress in transport. Mill owners objected to canals that reduced water-flow; land-owners feared for their fox coverts and some took direct action to oppose the construction of waterways, just as in the late 20th century proponents of road improvement or new airport runways clashed with environmentalists and local conservation groups. In the story of railway extension, there can be few more colourful incidents than the battle over Lord Harborough's curve.

76 / Leicestershire Events

69 *The building of the Midland Railway showing the Knighton Hills, the County Gaol, the Norwich Union building, then three separate private houses, and the bridge over Lancaster Road.*

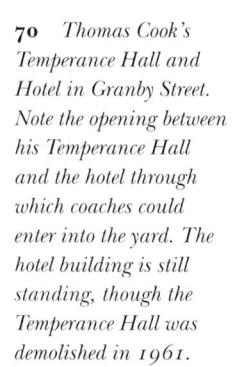

70 *Thomas Cook's Temperance Hall and Hotel in Granby Street. Note the opening between his Temperance Hall and the hotel through which coaches could enter into the yard. The hotel building is still standing, though the Temperance Hall was demolished in 1961.*

Harborough was one of the chief promoters of the Grantham canal and the tranquility of his estate at Stapleford was threatened by the proposed Peterborough and Midland Railway. For two days, the company's men met resistance from his lordship's staff as they attempted to survey the line. Then after a truce had been agreed for the matter to be taken before the magistrates, the rumour spread that the Railway men intended a surprise incursion in the early hours of the morning. The Company's men proceeded to arm themselves with staves and a bill hook, while Harborough's men 'procured wagons and strong hurdles as barricades, and a fire engine to pump on the enemy'. In an ultimatum to the Company's solicitors, Lord Harborough's representative warned: 'We have barricaded the towing-path, and have in readiness a few cannons from Lord Harborough's yacht. If you force us to use them, as a last resort, the blood be upon your heads.'

71-2 *Two of the panels on the offices of Thomas Cook erected in 1894 near the Clock Tower in Leicester. One shows an early train, with carriages open to the elements, passing through Charnwood on its way to the Temperance rally in Loughborough in 1841. The other depicts a later locomotive, taking visitors to the Great Exhibition at the Crystal Palace in 1851.*

73 *The Great Central at Stanford.*

74 *Some loads were too heavy and bulky to be carried by train, like this giant bell made for St Paul's Cathedral in London by Taylor's bell foundry in Loughborough. The foundry still exists and is one of the very last in the country.*

The Times reported that at about 7a.m. 'a party of nearly 100 men climbed over the park paling on the part nearest Oakham ... and commenced measuring with three or four chains'. As his Lordship's forces were spread over other points in the 800-acre estate, the men stationed at the scene were compelled to watch helplessly while the surveyors carried on with their work. When one of Harborough's tenants stood his ground, the battle began in earnest. The lock-keeper of the Oakham canal, 'a powerful man' sent his opponents 'head over heels at every blow; the noise was so great it was heard in the villages two miles off. The spikes of the railway

75 *The Bell, known as Great Paul, being transported to London. It is far larger than Big Ben. Three furnaces poured over 20 tons into the mould for its casting.*

76 *The Great Bell cast by Taylors of Loughborough arriving at St Paul's Cathedral in London.*

77 *Foxton Locks with the Lift on the Horizon.*

78 *By the turn of the century, traditional means of transport were facing new competition. The internal combustion engine was beginning to make its mark as the vehicle of the future and the electric tram was bringing a new means of popular transport to the towns. Here we see the tramlines being laid at the junction of London Road and Evington Road in Leicester.*

79 *The last horse-drawn tram at the Clock Tower in 1904.*

80 *A Hansom cab also passes the Clock Tower in the same year.*

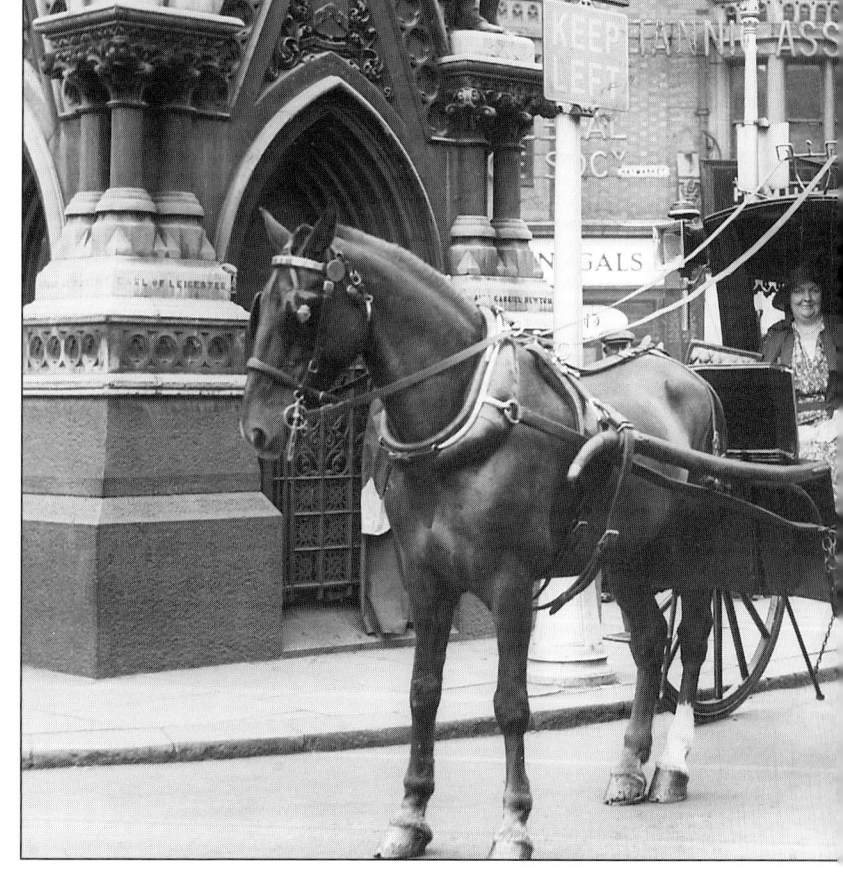

party were thrust into the sides of the defenders of the park, and after a battle of about five minutes, and many broken heads, wounded faces and sides, the lower grade of the intruders gave way.' The noise of the affray brought more parties of his Lordship's men to the scene and the 'railwayists' beat a retreat, 'their staves and chains having been broken into many pieces'.

There were threats of bringing more men to the aid of the Company but as 'the strength of his Lordship's [party] increased every minute from the villages of Freeby, Saxby, Wymondham, Whissendine, Teigh and other places, the day closed, leaving his Lordship in undisturbed possession of his park.'

Eventually, a compromise was reached whereby the railway line took a sharp turn to avoid encroaching on Stapleford Park. The stretch of line was known thereafter as 'Lord Harborough's curve'.

The last of the main railway trunk lines, the Manchester, Sheffield and Lincolnshire Railway, commonly known as the Great Central, was built in the 1890s. It is seen on page 77 in course of construction and at Stanford just to the north of Loughborough.

81 *Motor cars made their appearance during the 1890s such as this one at Cossington in 1897. It was made by Peberdy and Earp of Marlborough Street, Leicester.*

Mr Peberdy is seen on the right of the driver with Mr Earp behind him.

82 *From being a novelty and then a necessity the motor car has become a menace, an all-consuming threat to the peace of both town and countryside. It seems hard to credit that prior to 1958 Britain had no motorways and that in those days they still carried a certain stigma associated with the autobahns of Hitler's Germany. This picture captures the construction of the M1 as it passed through South Leicestershire. To the right of the road is the old Great Central line somewhere between Cosby and Lutterworth.*

The line closed in 1969, but part of it has been re-born as the Great Central Railway. Staffed by enthusiastic volunteers, it provides pleasure trips on the line between Loughborough and Birstall on the outskirts of Leicester. Its rolling stock and station platforms are often to be seen in period dramas on television and on the cinema screen.

Despite the limitations of road travel, compared with the speed of trains and the low cost of canals, roads were always essential for many purposes, and the road network grew as railways demanded feeder distribution networks.

Canals also kept their place in the overall provision of transport, but they fought a losing battle as freight increasingly chose the faster means of travel by rail. One obstacle to speed on the Leicestershire canals was the length of time taken to pass through the series of ten locks at Foxton. A brilliant piece of engineering designed to overcome this bottleneck was devised by Gordon Thomas, the canal company's engineer. It opened in 1900, using a steam engine to haul boats, floating in tanks of water, up an inclined plane built alongside the staircase of locks. Instead of taking an hour and a half to negotiate the locks, the Thomas lift enabled boats to pass through in eleven minutes. But, alas, the cost of working the lift was not covered by receipts from traffic, and the works were dismantled in 1927.

Aviation and Air Accidents

Early aeronautical events centred upon hot air balloons, and the county saw many of these during the 19th century, some more successful than others.

In 1864 one much-vaunted spectacle ended less in tragedy than in farce. A balloonist named Coxwell was about to make his ascent from Victoria Park, when a by-stander named Pegg, from Nottingham, seized hold of the basket and insisted on being taken aloft. This was out of the question as the added weight would have prevented lift-off, but the impatient crowd apparently supported Pegg, and when the balloonist deflated his gas bag to settle the matter, the crowd tore the balloon to shreds and set fire to the basket! Coxwell himself had to seek refuge at the home of Samuel Stone, the Town Clerk, who lived nearby on London Road, managing with difficulty to get inside Mr Stone's gate, but without one of his coat-tails.

More successful, though not especially novel or significant, was the balloonist, Dolly Shepherd, who entertained crowds at Ashby de la Zouch in 1908.

Had it not been for a fatal accident we might have boasted the Leicestershire origin of modern aviation, for Percy Pilcher made the last of his solo flights from Stanford Hall in the south of the county in 1899. He was born in 1866 and in 1895 he became the first man to make a controlled flight in the British Isles. Four years later, on 30 September 1899, he was staying at Stanford Hall where he demonstrated his latest glider, a triplane named the 'Hawk', to members of the Aeronautical Society. At about four

83 On 11 June 2003 an accident involving an Army transporter occurred on the M1 motorway near the junction with the M6. Eye-witnesses reported that a car lost control and careered across the north-bound carriageway hitting the transporter which then swerved and crashed through the central reservation into traffic going in the opposite direction. Five men were killed and both lanes were closed for 24 hours. The transporter was on its way back from Iraq to Catterick in North Yorkshire. It was an illustration of just how vulnerable the road network would be if such events were to be deliberately planned.

84 / LEICESTERSHIRE EVENTS

CORONATION BALLOON.

Under the Patronage of the Worshipful the Mayor.

MR. GREEN

RESPECTFULLY announces to the Inhabitants of Leicester and its vicinity, that he purposes, On MONDAY, July 26th, At Three o'clock in the Afternoon, making the Eighteenth

AERIAL VOYAGE,

From a commodious situation belonging to Mr. BRADLEY, adjoining the GAS WORKS.

Tickets of admission to witness the INFLATION, ATTACHING THE CAR, and LAUNCHING THE BALLOON, at 2s. and 3s. each, may be had of Mr. COMBE, Mr. CHAMBERLAIN, and Mr. COCKSHAW, Booksellers.

Bands of Music will attend, and Seats, with other accommodations will be provided.

ORDER OF SIGNALS.—A Gun will be fired to announce the commencement of Inflation; a second Gun will fired when the process is completed; and the Ascent will be notified by a third Gun and a Pilot Balloon.—To afford the Public as ample an opportunity as possible for inspecting the Balloon, the doors will be opened at Twelve o'clock.

o'clock in the afternoon, he launched his glider, using a horse-drawn pulley system. At the second attempt, the Hawk rose to about thirty feet when a sharp crack was heard and the tail appeared to give way. Pilcher flew about 200 yards before crashing in a field just over the county border in Northamptonshire. He never regained consciousness and died two days later.

Percy Pilcher's contribution to the history of aviation is not limited to his work on the 'Hawk' glider. He was working on a bi-plane fitted with an internal combustion engine when he died. Indeed, it was in order to demonstrate this powered-flight machine that he assembled his wealthy supporters at Stanford Hall in 1899. A technical problem caused him to shelve this intended aeroplane flight and to rely on his trusted 'Hawk' glider instead. Had he survived the accident to the glider, he might well have usurped the place of the Wright brothers in the history of flight.

By 1911 aviation was well established, and the *Daily Mail* sponsored a Circuit of Britain air race that incorporated a fuelling stop at Brentingby near Melton Mowbray. Huge crowds of onlookers came to catch a glimpse of the aeroplanes, straining to distinguish the machines from early birds at five o'clock in the morning. It was nearly eight in the evening before the last competitor passed over on his way to Edinburgh. So great was the interest among local school children that schools in Melton were closed for the day.

84 *Advertisement for a 'Coronation' balloon ascent in 1824.*

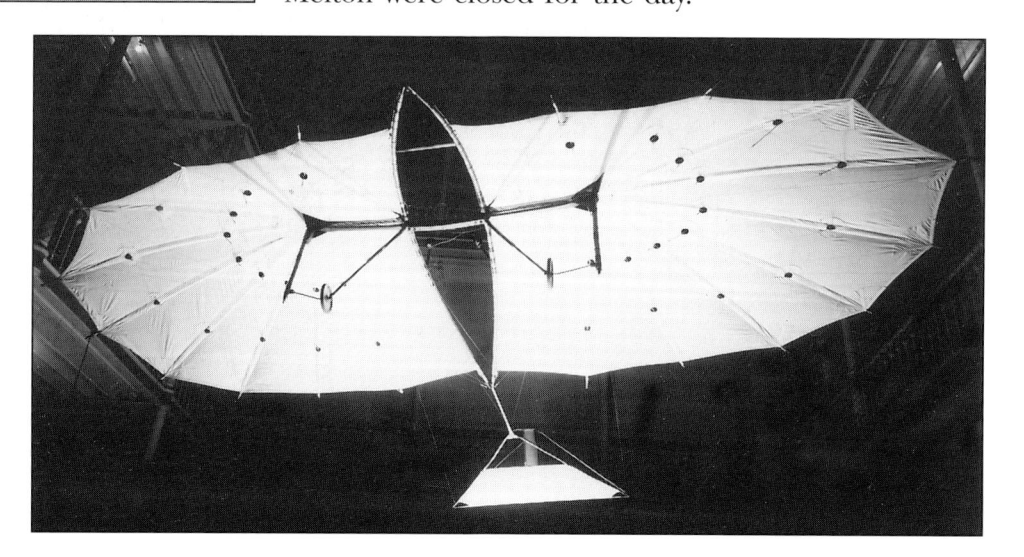

85 *Pilcher's original 'Hawk' glider, now in the National Museum of Flight, at Lothian, Edinburgh.*

The following year saw further contests and flying displays. The most famous aviator to visit Leicestershire was Gustav Hamel. Despite his name, he had been born in London in 1889 and was the first British pilot to fly between the capitals of France and England. He was also the first to carry mail from London to Windsor in 1911 and had given George V a private flying display.

At Hinckley, Hamel made several flights before crashing into a hedge. He himself was unharmed, but the machine, called after the French aviator Bleriot, was badly damaged in the propeller and port wing. Hamel had intended to fly over the county cricket ground where Leicestershire were playing the Australians. But at least he didn't land on the pitch.

86 *Gustav Hamel arriving at Loughborough in 1912, bringing the first-ever delivery of newspapers by air.*

87 *A 70hp Bleriot at Loughborough, taking part in the 1912* Daily Mail *Aero Circuit.*

88 *Taylorcraft Auster Mark 3.*

Again in 1912 Hamel achieved fame as the first man to deliver newspapers by air. He took off from the old cricket ground on Aylestone road on the morning of 30 November and deposited copies of *The Leicester Daily Post* to Loughborough. He was apparently numb with cold but he recovered sufficiently to give two exhibition flights later in the day.

By far the most significant episode in aeronautical engineering associated with the county was the development of the jet engine by Sir Frank Whittle and his team. Early experiments by Whittle's firm began in Rugby in 1936, and two years later the work moved to Lutterworth. Sir Frank Whittle records in his autobiography *Jet: The Story of a Jet Pioneer* that the activities of the firm were viewed with some suspicion by the local police, who thought they might have had IRA connections.

Like so many pioneers, Whittle had to contend with inadequate resources and the failure of others to recognise the importance of what he was doing. Working conditions were impossible, engineers sat and worked on stairs leading to the offices and a railway coach was hired to meet the need for more space. In the end he won through and, as we all know, changed the course of aviation history.

A chapter not so widely known is the development of Auster light aircraft and their contribution to the war effort from 1939 to 1945. The machines were made and tested at Rearsby.

During the Second World War, the 82nd Airborne division of the US army was stationed just outside Leicester at Stoughton Aerodrome. From here parachutists made practice flights, often landing in the fields of the neighbouring parishes. On one occasion, General Eisenhower visited the men at Stoughton, on 10 August 1944, to give them encouragement before the landings at Arnhem. A chunk of Charnwood granite stands on Victoria

Park in Leicester as a memorial to the American airmen who lost their lives during the campaign.

Sadly, in 1989, the county saw one of the worst air disasters of modern times. A Boeing 737, on a regular shuttle service between London Heathrow and Belfast, developed trouble in the left engine whilst approaching Derby. The crew had just started serving dinner when there was a repetitive thudding noise, and the aircraft began to vibrate. What looked like smoke poured into the cabin, and there was a strong smell of burning. Several passengers and crew members correctly identified the trouble as being located in the left engine, but the captain was misinformed by his first officer and shut down the good engine.

Fear mounted among the 156 passengers as the meal, only just served, was whisked away. The plane dropped so low that an attempt to restart the good engine had no chance of succeeding and the aircraft plunged into

89 *Auster Air Display at Rearsby.*

90 *A plane attempting an emergency landing at East Midlands airport crashed onto the embankment of the M1 leaving 47 dead and many more wounded.*

the side of the M1 motorway just short of Castle Donington aerodrome. 47 people died, and many more were seriously injured, though three crew members, and 13 of the passengers seated to the rear of the plane, escaped relatively unharmed.

The fact that so much is known about the accident and what caused it is due to the recovery of the flight recorder or 'black box'. Lessons learned at Kegworth were instrumental in avoiding similar accidents thereafter.

Nine
ACTS OF GOD

It seems a bit unfair that the Almighty should be associated with natural disasters, when sunshine and rain are so intermixed in the natural order of things. But we would soon tire of a catalogue of harvest festivals and happy holidays. The bad news is always on the front page, and the media hunts for human causes as well as human heroes and culprits. Only the insurance brokers really blame God.

An instance of just how complex the causes of tragic accidents may be, is found in the collapse of a building at the University of Leicester in 1983. The girders of the ferro-concrete roof apparently overlapped the supporting walls by a fraction of an inch and simply crashed under their own weight, but the timing of the collapse was surely an occasion for thanks giving. Had the event happened a week earlier, the Geography Department would have been full of students undertaking their final examinations, but, mercifully, the ceiling collapsed when no one was actually in the building. In fact, Colin Brooks, the University's Chief Photographer, to whom the author is indebted for producing many of the illustrations for this book, missed being the only casualty by five minutes – a lucky coffee-break indeed!

Here in the heart of the midlands we don't have cause to complain of high tides or coastal erosion, but there are occasional floods and fires. There are even the odd earth tremor and asteroid, but we know of no such events captured on camera. Acts of

91 *Collapse of the Geography Building at Leicester University in 1983.*

92 *South Croxton Church struck by lightning 1936.*

God are therefore confined here in the main to the scenes of devastation caused by accidental fire damage, as distinct from war damage, and to the effects of swollen rivers in time of heavy rain.

An instance of the damage that can be done when a building is struck by lightning, is seen in this view of South Croxton Church, which was severely damaged on 4 June 1936.

In November 1852 the Soar rose eight feet above its normal level, causing houses in low-lying areas to be flooded to four or five feet almost without warning. No lives were lost in Leicester, but a railway embankment was washed away at Loughborough, and at Wigston the river Sence burst through the embankment and severed the railway. It had all the makings of a major disaster, but the occcupant of the nearby Crow Mills rode into Wigston and Leicester in time to prevent any trains from crossing the viaduct.

Some places are naturally more prone to suffer flooding than others. The people of Ashby and Market Harborough are familiar with the tendency

ACTS OF GOD / 91

93 *Snow can also present problems as this sketch of drifts on the road to Market Harborough illustrates. It was drawn in 1888 and appeared in the* Illustrated London News.

94 *From the* Illustrated London News *comes this impression of the Crow Mills flood which swept away the railway bridge at South Wigston in 1852.*

95 *Market Harborough, awash with water in December 1900. To the eastern side of the county, the Eye and the Wreake pose occasional problems for Melton Mowbray, as in December 1900 when this photograph recorded flooding in Burton Street.*

96 *Floods in Melton Mowbray in 1900.*

of water levels to rise as melting snow and heavy rain cause flash floods, as are those who live in villages of the Soar valley, such as Sileby, Syston and Quorn. In the cemetery at Sileby is a memorial to three local boys who were skating from Sileby to Cossington in 1891, when they fell through the ice and drowned. A similar fate met three boys from Aylestone who were skating in January 1897.

Market Harborough grew as a crossing point on the river Welland and, as a low-lying settlement, has always known the danger of flooding. On St Swithin's Day, 1880, the church was flooded to a depth of three feet; twenty years later the floods were almost as bad.

In so far as we build our homes near rivers liable to flood, we have only ourselves to blame when periodic inundation follows, but storm and flood waters are clearly natural disasters beyond our control. Fire hazards, on the other hand, are invariably the consequence of human carelessness. Even the occasional bush fire in high summer generally has its origin in a dropped cigarette.

97 *Inundation at Ashby de la Zouch in May 1925 was the result of a sudden torrential storm. Here we see Market Street flooded to four feet.*

Fires that get out of control are too common to be classed as events, but they become noteworthy as the scale of destruction increases. Of all natural disasters, fire tends to be the most calamitous. The process of change is rapid and dramatic, imprinting itself on the memory as familiar landmarks suddenly disappear. An event such as the destruction of St George's church, Leicester, in October 1911, made just such a distinct impression on a whole generation.

November 2002 saw the beginning of a long strike by the fire-fighters union. The dangerous nature of their profession was only too clearly illustrated by a factory fire in Morledge Street, off Humberstone Gate, Leicester, when a fireman was killed. Robert Miller died while tackling a fire in a disused factory near the centre of Leicester.

The death of one fireman brought home to millions the real danger inherent in the work undertaken by members of the Fire Brigades Union.

98 *The Brush works in Loughborough in December 1910. A horse-drawn carriage negotiating the turn into the works through floodwater.*

ACTS OF GOD / 95

99 *Floods at the junction of Ashby Road and Derby Road, Loughborough in the 1930s.*

100 *A flooded road at Dishley in August 1912. The horse-drawn carriage shows its ability to cope with the situation, while a motor car is stranded.*

101 *A charabanc driving through water on Derby Road, Ashby de la Zouch, 1925.*

Likewise, the deaths of coal miners serve to remind the community at large of the risks borne by men extracting coal from deep below ground. The mining community of Coalville experienced the trauma of collective grief in 1898, when fire swept through underground galleries of Whitwick mine, causing the deaths of 35 men.

The death-rate in 19th-century pits fell as safer methods of working were introduced, but accidents still happened even into the last days of coal mining. No one can regret the passing of a way of life so arduous and unhealthy as the mining of coal underground, but Leicestershire mines enjoyed prosperity, and there were generally better relations between coal owners and men at the coal face than elsewhere.

Coal has been mined in Leicestershire since at least the 12th century, at first from bell-pits, the remains of which can still be traced on the ground near Swannington, and later by sinking shafts and tunnelling into the seams. The long-wall system of mining used at Whitwick entailed cutting coal for a distance of thirty yards before the emptied space was filled in with waste material. Great care was taken to support the roof of these seams but the pressure was immense. The consequent settling and subsidence of strata above such mine workings is frequently visible above ground in the damage to housing by subsidence.

102 *Occasionally, absence of water can present us with difficulties, such as water shortages through the drying-up of reservoirs. This view of Swithland in 1929 is given added interest by the presence of three motorists admiring the unfamiliar scene.*

Areas left after the coal was extracted in the depths of the mine were known as 'gobs', and it is thought that spontaneous combustion in air pockets within one of these gobs led to the fire at Whitwick. Men trapped underground would often die from the effects of gas known as 'fire stink'. The healthier the men, the more likely they were to breathe deeply and to succumb, so that it was remarked that only the more puny miners escaped alive.

One survivor left this account of his ordeal:

> It all came so suddenly that we had no time to think. We all called to one another and I got hold of my father ... by his right arm, and my brother, who was with us, took hold of his left arm. The smoke was dense and blinding, while the heat was also

103 *In Elmesthorpe, on 11 May 1914, a fire destroyed one of the Countess Lovelace's cottages. Note the railway dray in the foreground. The dray is inscribed as belonging to 'the London North Western Midland Railways C Section Elmesthorpe Station.'*

very great. We dragged each other along; we rushed into the smoke and fire, and I kept pulling and pulling with all my might. I cannot tell you exactly how it was, but something seemed to be holding my father back. We kept pulling and pulling him till I could do no more. I was quite exhausted. It seemed after we had linked arms that we would get through, but we became so exhausted that we got parted. I caught hold of my father again, but could not move him, and I staggered through. I left my father and brother ...

However arduous they were, conditions in the pits were well-known and had been subject to parliamentary control since 1842, but in other trades, regulation was hampered by the widespread and small-scale nature of industrial units. Children were peculiarly at risk, since they had no trade

ACTS OF GOD / 99

104-5 *Scenes at the pit head. Anxious crowds awaiting news of men trapped in the Whitwick colliery disaster of 1898.*

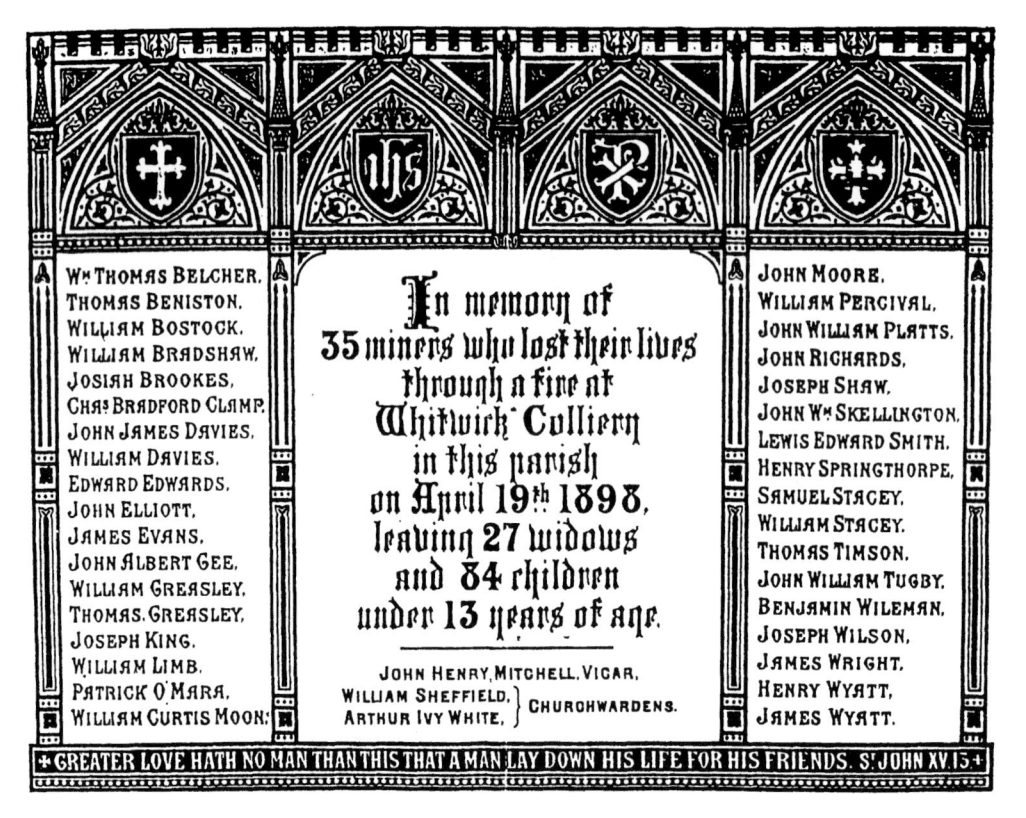

106 *The memorial tablet in Whitwick church.*

unions to back them and they were often cruelly exploited. The fate of the brick-yard children in north-west Leicestershire was a case in point. George Smith of Coalville made it his life's work to expose this exploitation and to bring the brick-yards under government inspection. As a result of his exposure of conditions in the brick-yards, a clause was added to the Factory Act of 1871 prohibiting child labour in this trade.

Lord Shaftesbury spoke in favour of the clause, describing the conditions in which the children worked from his own observations in the brick-yards:

> I saw little children three parts naked, tottering under the weight of wet clay—some of it on their heads and some on their shoulders - and little girls with large masses of wet cold, and dripping clay pressed on their abdomens. Moreover, the unhappy children were exposed to the most sudden transitions of heat and cold, for after carrying their burdens of wet clay they had to endure the heat of the kiln, and to enter places where the heat was so fierce that I was not myself able to remain there more than two or three minutes.

Smith went on to campaign with equal energy for the offspring of canal boat people, again with surprising success, but even he was defeated when he tried to bring children of the travelling Romanies into the ambit of the education acts.

ACTS OF GOD / 101

107 *A young worker in the brick-yards.*

Ten
CIVIC AND ROYAL EVENTS

Pomp and ceremony have their role to play in the affairs of town and village life just as they do in matters of state. The annual mayoral show or the beating of the bounds of country parishes and the decking of the maypole are as important to the collective identity of village and town as the State Opening of Parliament or the Changing of the Guard to the nation as a whole. But the grandeur of civic ceremonial quickly fades into insignificance and the parades and paraphernalia of the past can seem pompous and even ridiculous.

As with fox-hunting and church-going, devotion to the monarchy declined markedly in the 20th century. In the time of Victoria, the Queen's longevity provided two great occasions for national exuberance and the subsequent coronations of her son and grandson gave further excuse for effusions of loyalty and jollification.

108 *Ashby de la Zouch celebrates Queen Victoria's Golden Jubilee in 1887.*

CIVIC AND ROYAL EVENTS / 103

The expansion of industrial towns in the 19th century brought new and daunting challenges to those responsible for local government. Previous generations had rarely concerned themselves with anything more than managing corporate property and the administration of local charities but, as numbers swelled, the need for social intervention became increasingly apparent. Policing was one aspect of communal life where something had to be done, and we have already noted the establishment of the local police forces in town and county. What to do with the poor was another matter that led to intervention on a vast scale. Workhouses, deliberately forbidding and intentionally austere, were built to house those who could not, for whatever reason, make ends meet. But there were other, more positive, responses to urban growth. Some wealthy philanthropists endowed schools, parks and

109 *Jubilant crowds, bandsmen and rifle volunteers celebrate in Ashby de la Zouch, 1887.*

110 *Preparing for the band to play during Jubilee celebrations at Ashby de la Zouch, 1887.*

111 *At Loughborough the Market Place festooned and thronged with people for the Jubilee celebrations, 1887.*

reading rooms or built churches for the spiritual benefit of the poor. Sometimes the town councillors also saw the need for education, culture and enlightenment for those without means to afford their own provision.

Leicester Corporation was well in the van of progress in such matters. The town had the first municipal park in the country, albeit a rather forlorn piece of ground next to the prison, now called Nelson Mandela Park, but it was set aside for public recreation in 1839, long before that at Birkenhead, which claims the distinction of being the first publicly-provided park.

The Council also provided some of the first public baths on New Walk in 1846, the same year in which its Medical Officers were appointed, three months before the celebrated Dr Duncan in Liverpool, and in 1849 it turned its attention to the creation of a public cemetery and a museum.

CIVIC AND ROYAL EVENTS / 105

112 *Planting a tree in Leicester's Victoria Park to mark the Queen's Diamond Jubilee in 1897.*

113 *The Market Place in Loughborough, showing Edward VII's coronation in 1902.*

21 June 1849 saw a double event in the civic story of Leicester. Both Welford Road cemetery and the museum on New Walk were officially opened on that day. The cemetery was something of a triumph for the Corporation, as inter-denominational rivalry had threatened to scupper any proposed scheme. In the event the cemetery was divided between the Anglican and Nonconformist sections to the satisfaction of everyone.

The original collection of exhibits in the New Walk museum came from the Leicester Literary and Philosophical Society, which had started in 1835. The building had been erected as a private school in 1837 for sons of free-churchmen, who refused to send their offspring to the Anglican Collegiate School in Prebend Street. When the school closed, the imposing classical building was purchased by the Corporation and became one of the first municipal museums in the country. Four decades later, the Corporation built a new Art School adjacent to the Museum.

Some of the colour went out of civic ceremony in Leicester with the triumph of the radicals in the early 19th century. The cost-cutting Council sold off not only the town plate and dinner services but even the maces

LORD NELSON
BAXTER GATE
BAPTIST
PRIMITIVE METHODIST
SUNDAY SCHOOLS
LOUGHBOROUGH

108 / LEICESTERSHIRE EVENTS

114 *In Charnwood forest at Beacon Hill, a huge bonfire, 40 feet high, was lit in honour of Edward's accession.*

115 *Festivities marking the coronation of George V in Market Street, Ashby de la Zouch, in 1911.*

fashioned in the reign of Charles II to replace those pillaged by his father's forces during the Civil War. The Mayor did without a mayoral chain till one holder of that office found himself debarred from entry to a royal reception in London, because he wasn't wearing the customary badge of office. The Council agreed forthwith to commission a new chain to save any future embarrassment. (Council Minutes 1867 LRO CM1/11 p144)

A reminder of civic life before the reform of political institutions in Victoria's reign is in the pictures on page 114 of a parliamentary election in 1826. Voting was done in the open, because secret ballots were regarded as un-English if not cowardly. How men voted, however, might reflect the quantity of ale provided and, if they failed to vote as their employers or landlords wished, they might well find themselves out of a job and with no roof over their heads. Not till 1870 was the Ballot Act passed, giving this essential freedom from intimidation to the individual voter.

116 *A civic procession passing along Granby Street in Loughborough as part of its coronation celebrations in 1911.*

117 *At Market Harborough, the children were presented with commemorative mugs for the coronation of George V in 1911.*

Queen Victoria once visited Belvoir Castle, returning through Leicester to board the train to London, but she did not stay in the county town. Perhaps, like her loquacious prime minister, William Gladstone, she was far too busy with affairs of state. When pressed by his loyal supporters to come and open the town's new Liberal Club, in 1887, Gladstone took three quarters of an hour to explain to the member for Leicester why he had no time to spare for such a visit.

The Prince of Wales and Princess Alexandra were, however, prevailed upon to come to Leicester in 1882 on the occasion of the official opening of Abbey Park. For the Prince of Wales, it was the second time he had visited Leicester that year, for, in January 1882, he had come to shoot game on Lord Stamford's estate at Bradgate. The earl was then living at Groby in the second Bradgate House, built in 1856 and demolished in 1926. Enthusiastic crowds followed the royal coach on a way lined with lanterns and rockets, and the party had the satisfaction of killing 2,000 birds the following day.

Prior to the opening of Abbey Park, elaborate preparations were made for the royal visitors. Six thousand school children watched the presentation of a loyal address in the Market Place, before the whole company made its way, through excited crowds and beneath triumphal arches in Belgrave Gate, to the park, where the Princess planted a commemorative oak tree. The day ended with fireworks reflected in the still surface of the river Soar.

CIVIC AND ROYAL EVENTS / 111

Every effort was made to ensure the success of the day, but one man got a little too excited, mixing alcohol with patriotic fervour, and attempted to shake hands with the Princess as she passed by Dover Street. He was quickly bundled off to the police station and sentenced next day to a week's hard labour. When news of his imprisonment reached the ears of the royal visitors, the Prince at once sent a letter to the Mayor urging clemency, and His Worship accordingly asked for the prisoner to be released. However, the Prison Governor was at the dentist's at the time the request was granted and, when he heard of the release of his prisoner, was somewhat put out. Once detained in gaol a prisoner should only be freed by direct intervention of the sovereign or by order of the Home Secretary.

118 *The coronation of George V in 1911 celebrated in Loughborough.*

112 / Leicestershire Events

119 *Typical of the local celebrations that brought colour and excitement to rural communities were the annual commemorations of Empire Day and of May Day. Here the inhabitants of Kibworth enjoy May Day in 1908. The event was evidently an opportunity to see and admire the latest automobile.*

The Mayoral faux-pas was put right by a retrospective order later in the day and Charles Walkerdine retained his liberty. There was a rather touching letter to the Mayor's wife from the Princess, disclaiming the notion that she had suffered in any way and denying rumours that she had hit the man with her umbrella.

> Dear Mrs Chambers,
> I cannot rest until I have told you how distressed I am at the report which has been spread everywhere that I was annoyed by the poor man who tried to shake hands with me and that I consequently hit him with my parasol. On the contrary, I was so horrified at the rough way in which he was handled, and fearing that the officer's horse would tread on him, I put out my parasol to protect him.

CIVIC AND ROYAL EVENTS / 113

120 *Cemetery Chapels in Welford Road Cemetery.*

121 *Mary Linwood.*

122 An Exhibition of Fine Art held to celebrate the Opening of the New School of Art in New Walk, January 1885. Among the collections of Leicester Museum are some of the needlework designs of Miss Mary Linwood. She enjoyed phenomenal fame in her own day but always refused to sell her work despite being offered three thousand guineas for one of them. She exhibited in London and Paris, where Napoleon sat for her. The resulting portrait is now displayed in the British gallery of the Victoria and Albert Museum. Mary Linwood died at the age of 90 in 1845.

123 *The Hustings at the election of 1826.*

124 *Close of Poll in the Market Place 1826.*

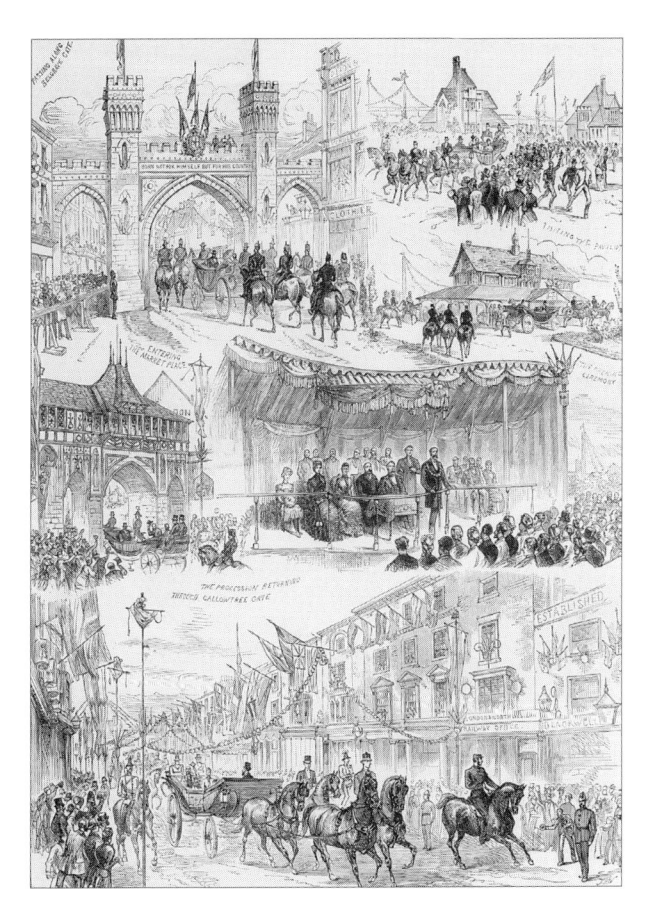

Immediately the Prince and myself heard that he had actually been imprisoned for his supposed offence we telegraphed to your husband to beg the poor man might be instantly released, and we were so glad that our request was granted.

I must take this opportunity of repeating how touched we were by the most kind and hearty reception we met with in your beautiful town of Leicester, and I assure you that the 29th of May will ever be engraven on our memory as one of the brightest and pleasantest of our lives.

Believe me
Dear Mrs Chambers
Yours truly
Alexandra

125 *(top left) The Prince and Princess of Wales open Abbey Park, 29 May 1882.*

126 *(top right) Princess Alexandra planting an oak tree in Abbey Park.*

In the years before the First World War there was increasing acrimony over the issue of votes for women. The Women's Social and Political Union had offices in Bowling Green Street, Leicester, and many members of the most prominent families in the town supported its activities. They were for the most part peaceful and law-abiding in their protests, but some women, tired of the slow progress of their cause, took to arson as a means of protest. Stoughton Grange was the subject of one such attack.

The War saw a seismic shift in political affiliations. The once invincible party of Lloyd George was riven with personal animosity and fatally compromised by its coalition with the Tories. The Labour Party, on the other hand, had grown in confidence and in the experience of shared power. Ramsay Macdonald, who sat for Leicester from 1906 to 1918, formed his first Labour government in 1924. During the preceding election campaign, Winston Churchill fought his last fight as a member of the Liberal Party. He was beaten by Major Pethwick Lawrence, the Labour candidate and husband of a prominent suffragette.

Memorials to those who died in the First World War can be found in almost every village and town in England. They record events which were as cataclysmic for the bereaved as they were horrendous for those who fought in the trenches. The Leicester memorial, designed by Sir Edwin Lutyens, has immense dignity. Richard Gill writes of its 'subtle avoidance of triumphalism'. 'One can feel', he says, of its huge arch, 'the plangent emptiness of grief and loss. It is a monument in which deep emotions are controlled by the sublimities of art.'

In Queen's Park, Loughborough, there is a unique memorial in the shape of a bell tower, 150ft high, and a Carillon of 47 bells, cast in Loughborough at the works of John Taylor and Company. They range in weight from 20 lbs to over four tons. Sir Edward Elgar composed a Memorial Chime for the ceremony marking completion of the memorial in 1923.

Had Leicester retained its abbey at the Dissolution, it would almost certainly have become a cathedral city much earlier. An unsuccessful attempt to acquire city status was made in 1889, when the Mayor instigated a petition to the Queen. It made the point that Leicester was referred to in Domesday Book as a City. It had its own see in AD 679 but lost it with the Danish conquest of AD 877. Henry VIII toyed with the idea of turning the abbey into a cathedral, but decided against it, and attempts in Victoria's time to elevate the town to the status of a city proved fruitless.

It was not till 1919 that Leicester was recognised as such, and it was ten years later before it had its own cathedral. There was then a great debate as to which of the ancient churches should be chosen to fill this role. Probably the original Saxon cathedral had been at the church of St Nicholas. All Saints also had its advocates and, to many minds, the finest and most awesome interior belongs to St Margaret's. But St Martin's church has the merit of being both large and centrally placed, adjacent to the Guildhall and in the heart of the old town, and it was consequently elevated to the status of a cathedral in 1929.

For many Leicester folk, the Clock Tower is, in the words of the late Professor W.G.Hoskins, 'the hub of the town—or indeed of the universe'. But it is in fact a fairly modern structure, placed where it is as a sort of pedestrian refuge. After the removal of the remains of the old Assembly rooms from the East Gates site, there was a rather perilous convergence of five main roads at this part of Leicester. What was needed was 'an island

CIVIC AND ROYAL EVENTS / 117

127 *Lutyens' War Memorial in Victoria Park, Leicester.*

128 *The Carillon at Loughborough and crowds gathering at the opening ceremony in 1934. It still plays every Thursday at one o'clock and for special concerts in the summer.*

129 *Laying the foundation stone of the Clock Tower, 1868.*

of sanctuary and security – somewhere to stand to prevent people being run over crossing the street'.

What may well be the first traffic census of modern times was conducted here on 23 November 1861, between 8 a.m. and 10 p.m., to add some statistical weight to the argument. A total of 54,300 pedestrians passed the East Gates road junction, together with 2,960 vehicles with 5,900 drivers and passengers. In addition horses, cattle, sheep and pigs were in evidence but no details were recorded.

John Burton, an enterprising photographer whose premises overlooked the site, suggested a competition to devise an ornamental structure containing four illuminated clock dials and four statuettes of benefactors of the town that would act as a traffic-island or place of safety for passing pedestrians. After a somewhat acrimonious contest, the competition was won by Joseph Goddard, for his Gothic design, 'bristling with canopies and wavy with crockets', which was considered more modern than its rivals. The Goddard family have the distinction of producing a dynasty of architects, six generations of which Joseph was the third.

A 'demolition dinner' was held in June 1862 to mark the removal of the old Assembly rooms and, six years later on 16 March 1868, John Burton laid the foundation stone of the Clock Tower. The work was completed in 12 weeks which, of course, merited another celebratory dinner, and the scaffolding was removed, on 18 July, to coincide with the holding of the Royal Agricultural Show in Leicester.

If the Clock Tower has always been regarded with affection, the same cannot be said of Leicester's Civic Centre. It was built as a speculative venture in office accommodation on the site of the Wolsey hosiery factory. When the City Council proposed buying it for their own needs in 1975, all hell was let loose. The local paper, the *Leicester Mercury*, ran a campaign against the waste of public money involved, five and a quarter million pounds. But in retrospect it all seems to have been a bit irrational. Given that the Council offices had been scattered throughout the city and were easily accommodated in the two central blocks, the money appears to have been well spent.

The mid-Victorian period saw a great rise in the number of schools and educational institutions of all kinds. Here we see the ceremonial opening

130 *The Opening Ceremony for Loughborough Endowed School, from the* Illustrated London News, *1850.*

131 *Loughborough Grammar School opened 1850.*

of the new Loughborough Endowed School in 1850. The funds originated in a bequest of Thomas Burton, a merchant of the Staple in 1498, who was a native and resident of Loughborough. 104 tables were each set for 24 children to enjoy a celebratory feast.

Victorian enthusiasm for engineering equalled that for education. People took enormous pride in the achievements of architects and builders and even the most mundane structures were celebrated as evidence of progress and civilisation. In 1895, the Corporation of Leicester marked the completion of their new sewerage irrigation system at Beaumont Leys by a ceremonial dinner held in the bell mouth of the sewer itself!

132 *Celebratory dinner in the bell mouth of the new sewer, 1895. The quality of this photograph is poor, but it is so unusual to see a celebratory dinner in a sewer that it is included here.*

Eleven
SOCIAL EVENTS

During the early 18th century smallpox was the most dreaded of all diseases. The death toll was often horrendous as, for example, after an outbreak on the Scottish island of Foula, where only six out a population of over two hundred remained to bury the dead. Inoculation against the disease was advocated by Lady Mary Wortley Montagu, who had seen its positive benefits in Turkey in 1719. By the mid-century it was being used on a wide scale, long before Jenner's adoption of vaccination—that is, using cow pox instead of the human form of the disease to inoculate against it.

Many people were unconvinced that introducing the infected matter from a cow would benefit them or their children, and this scepticism led in Leicester to a full-scale rebellion against governmental attempts to enforce vaccination. The National Anti-Vaccination League had its headquarters in the town, and huge demonstrations were held in protest against compulsory vaccination. Monday, 23 March 1885 saw 80,000 to 100,000 filling the market place, the biggest demonstration ever known in Leicester, with contingents from all over the country and from overseas. Among 700 banners and flags, one urged: 'Men of Kent defend your liberty of conscience; better a felon's cell than a poisoned babe'; the Keighley banner declared 'We fight for our homes and liberty' and another simply demanded 'Sanitation, not Vaccination'.

The government remained unmoved and vaccination proceeded almost everywhere except in Leicester, where thousands were prosecuted for non-compliance with the Vaccination Acts. By 1897 only 1.3 per cent of the children in Leicester were vaccinated, and the local Board of Guardians, whose job it was to administer the Vaccination Acts, refused to appoint an officer to carry out the work. Threatened with prison, they eventually gave way, but Leicester remained resolutely opposed to the practice of vaccination for the next three decades.

For the most part, anti-vaccinators could point to Leicester's freedom from smallpox as a vindication of their view that vaccination was ineffective and unnecessary, though their opponents could state, equally fairly, that the vaccination of the rest of the country was a principal cause of the town's immunity. Whatever the truth of these assertions, there is no doubt that, by rejecting the needle, the town's sanitary authorities were more inclined to pursue other lines of defence against disease. The city fathers put their faith instead into rigourous cleaning of the streets, isolation of suspected sufferers and attacking what were seen as the environmental causes of disease; hence the slogan 'Sanitation not Vaccination'.

The beginning of the 20th century saw a good deal of industrial unrest. Unemployment was often high and prices rising, while competition from abroad was already eating into the industrial supremacy that Britain enjoyed in the early years of Victoria's reign. Neither Unemployment Benefit nor Old Age Pensions were yet on the political horizon, and desperate poverty was still evident despite the general rise in living standards.

A voluntary social worker reported on one of several visits to the homes of the poor in Leicester in January 1905: 'We entered a dark room with a cracked uneven floor. Broken panes of glass, mended with paper and pieces of board, were in the window frame. A couple of boxes against the wall formed a rude couch. A woman, evidently ill with bronchitis, lay there, covered with a ragged coat.' When the husband emerged, he was gaunt and unshaven, 'with a face as pale and haggard as the countenance of the dead. He spoke feverishly, as if he were losing all self-control. "I don't want your relief tickets", he said. "I want work. What the unemployed man wants is not charity, but enough work to support himself and his family."'

Added to the sense of despair was the ubiquitous horror of 'going on the parish' or becoming a pauper. The conviction that receiving any kind of state help was degrading and shameful stemmed from the Poor Law Amendment Act of 1834. Those who framed the Act had drummed into the consciousness of the entire nation a rooted belief in the moral depravity of any unfortunate enough to seek relief in the work-house—the 'bastilles' of the Poor Law Unions.

Against this background some four hundred men set out to walk from Leicester to London in the hope of presenting their case to Parliament and to the King. They were led by a cycle shop owner, Amos Sherriff, and by the vicar of St Mark's Church, Belgrave Gate, in Leicester.

The Rev. F. Lewis Donaldson had come to his working-class parish in 1896 after a year in the colliery village of Nailstone. He was a passionate believer in Christian Socialism. Before the march, he wrote to the Archbishop of Canterbury urging him to show some sympathy with the men by meeting some of them personally. The Archbishop declined, and Donaldson published their correspondence. In his reply Donaldson wrote, 'if a few words of sympathy with their want of work, and therefore of food, could have been given them by your Grace in person, it would have done much to comfort them, and, through them, thousands of others in their condition throughout England. Also it would have done much to disabuse their minds of the idea, widely prevalent amongst them, that the tragedy and pathos of their condition is neither apprehended by the English Church, nor regarded by the Church as a matter with which she is most deeply concerned.'

Donaldson's open rebuke to his superior is thought to have cost him a bishopric, but he was never a man to compromise or take the easy way. The men never met the King or cabinet, but their march was well-covered by the press and may have had some effect upon the passing of the Unemployed Workmen's Act in the following year.

There are few politicians of national importance who were born in Leicestershire. Of those who sat for constituencies in the city or county, Ramsay MacDonald later became Prime Minister but not while he was based in Leicester. Stephen Dorrell sat as the member for Loughborough South while in Mrs Thatcher's government, and Patricia Hewitt, the Secretary for Trade and Industry, is member for West Leicester, but neither of them was born in the county. Lord Lawson sat for the Blaby constituency from 1974 to 1992 and was Chancellor of the Exchequer for six years, from 1983 to 1989. Every Budget Day saw the press descend upon his home village of Blaby to capture a shot of the man behind the dispatch box.

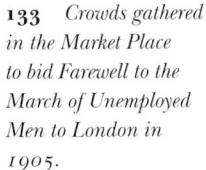

133 *Crowds gathered in the Market Place to bid Farewell to the March of Unemployed Men to London in 1905.*

134 *The men stopping overnight at Market Harborough, bedding down on straw in the Cattle Market.*

Leicestershire has a long and proud history of religious diversity. Mention has been made of the expulsion of the Jews by Simon de Montfort but, in later times, Leicester was the first town in Britain to elect a Jewish mayor, Sir Israel Hart, a bluff hearty man whose fortune was based in ready-made tailoring. His firm, Hart and Levy, had a string of retail outlets known as Grand Clothing Halls in several northern towns as well as that in Leicester. The Leicester branch now forms the High Street entrance to The Shires shopping mall.

Mount St Bernard's was the first monastery to be built in England since the Reformation. It was a visible sign of the growing strength of Catholicism and its threat to Protestantism. It was funded largely by the Earl of Shrewsbury and begun in 1840 to the design of A.W.N. Pugin, though it was not finished till a century later in 1939, and Pugin's original designs were much modified.

The presence of the new monastery excited a good deal of suspicion and hostility at the time. It was seen as part of an attack upon Protestant Christianity and the giving of alms by the monks was said to encourage begging in the county. Leicestershire had a long established antipathy to the Church of Rome. John Wycliffe was at Lutterworth, when he lit the first candle of protest against Catholic Christendom. George Fox, the Quaker, hailed from Leicestershire, as did the Countess of Huntingdon in the late 18th century. The most powerful force within the Protestant fold in Leicestershire was, however, evident in the numerical strength of the Baptists.

It was from a small cottage near the West Bridge that William Carey set out to spread Christianity in India in the late 18th century. Several other Leicester Baptists, such as Robert Hall, had a reputation for oratory and

135 *Monks building at St Bernard's Abbey in Charnwood Forest in the 1930s.*

religious fervour that went way beyond the borders of the county. Harvey Lane Baptist Chapel had to be enlarged several times to accommodate the huge congregations attracted by Robert Hall, and the Baptist chapel in Belvoir Street, built in 1845 to the designs of the Roman Catholic architect, Joseph Hansom, accommodated 1,500 people.

Attendance at church services remained high until 1914 and patriotic sentiment kept allegiance to the church strong until the end of the Great War, but, in the 20th century, rationalism and the pull of other interests tended to erode belief and religious observance, so that by the end of the century many churches were empty, abandoned and even demolished. None of this was true of the new immigrant communities, for many of whom religious observance is seen as vital to their cultural identity.

Several city churches now cater predominantly for those who came originally from the West Indies, such as the Seventh Day Adventists who worship in the former Victoria Road Baptist church. Sikhs and Hindus now worship in former Christian churches, such as the Baptist Church on

136 *The Baptist Chapel on Belvoir Street, from the* Illustrated London News *1845.*

> **AN IMPORTANT ANNOUNCEMENT ON BEHALF OF THE COUNCIL OF THE CITY OF LEICESTER, ENGLAND**
>
> from the "Uganda Argus" 29.9.1972
>
> The City Council of Leicester, England, believe that many families in Uganda are considering moving to Leicester. If YOU are thinking of doing so it is very important you should know that PRESENT CONDITIONS IN THE CITY ARE VERY DIFFERENT FROM THOSE MET BY EARLIER SETTLERS. They are:-
>
> **HOUSING** — several thousands of families are already on the Council's waiting list.
>
> **EDUCATION** — hundreds of children are awaiting places in schools.
>
> **SOCIAL AND HEALTH SERVICES** — already stretched to the limit.
>
> **IN YOUR OWN INTERESTS AND THOSE OF YOUR FAMILY YOU SHOULD ACCEPT THE ADVICE OF THE UGANDA RESETTLEMENT BOARD AND NOT COME TO LEICESTER**

137 Advertisement which was placed in the Uganda Argus *in 1972 in an attempt to stem the influx of refugees from East Africa into Leicester.*

Clarendon Park Road, Leicester. In 1988, the former Congregational chapel in Oxford Street became the only Jain temple, with consecrated images, outside India, apart from two in Kenya. It is lavishly decorated in white marble, much of it sent from India at great expense.

The lights celebrating Diwali are said to be the most spectacular outside London. Leicester's Belgrave Mela takes place every year in Abbey Park. Begun in 1983 as the Belgrave Carnival to give encouragement to local individuals and group entertainers in the predominantly Asian neighbourhood of Belgrave, the celebration changed its name to the Belgrave Mela, a traditional Indian festival held at the end of harvest, in 1986. Promoting Asian arts and culture of all kinds, it still focuses on local talent in the neighbourhood but it now attracts visitors from all over the country.

Leicester's Caribbean Carnival is second only to that of Notting Hill in the calendar of West Indian annual events in Britain. It has been celebrated each year since 1984 with enormous enthusiasm, bringing song, dance, colour and Caribbean cuisine to the huge crowds that gather in Victoria Park. Innovative costumes illustrate different themes in the Carnival procession that tours the city centre prior to the crowning of the Carnival Queen. The festivities culminate in a grand Carnival Mama, Queen, Prince and Princess show in the De Montfort Hall.

There can hardly have been a more momentous event in the last half-century than the expulsion of Asian people from East Africa. When Idi Amin began his programme of 'Africanisation', expelling all those of Indian origin from Uganda, the horror of what was taking place was literally incredible. We all thought that such barbarism had reached its climax in Nazi Germany with the murder of millions in the gas chambers, but, alas, it has become all too familiar under the euphemism of 'ethnic cleansing'.

In the 1970s, Leicestershire people were more aware of what was happening in central Africa than most of their fellow countrymen. Thousands of desperate Uganda Asians fled from their homeland with virtually nothing but the clothes on their backs. At that time Leicester Corporation was engaged in a housing regeneration programme that involved whole streets of Victorian houses, in the Belgrave district, north of the city. Consequently, there were hundreds of houses awaiting demolition that could be bought at very low prices. These acted as a magnet to impoverished refugees and, as more and more arrived, they too were drawn to the streets off Belgrave Road and Humberstone Road.

Leicester's Asian quarter has now spread over much of the city and Leicester is set to become the first

138 *Diwali is the Hindu festival of Light, which takes place each year. A young girl holds a diva lamp during Diwali in 2003.*

139 *Mosque in Evington Road. One of several large and imposing mosques in different parts of the city and county.*

140 *Dancers at the Caribbean Carnival on Victoria Park in 2001.*

large town or city in Britain in which black and Asian people outnumber the indigenous population. Whatever our initial reaction to the newcomers, familiarity bred, not contempt, but understanding. Neighbours became friends and workmates became pals. Leicester is now a truly multi-cultural community. We celebrate diversity. Different religions and cultural practices add vibrancy to a city that likes to boast itself 'full of surprises', and Leicester's old Latin motto '*semper eadem*'—always the same—seems ever more obsolete in the 21st century.

Select Bibliography

Bailey, Brian, *Portrait of Leicestershire* (1977)
Bonser, Roy, *Aviation in Leicestershire and Rutland* (2001)
Bristow, Adrian, *George Smith, the Children's Friend* (1999)
Crane, Arthur, *The Kirkland Papers* (1990)
East, C. Wendy, *The Green Bicycle Mystery* (1993)
Elliott, Malcolm, *Victorian Leicester* (1979)
Ellis, Colin, *History in Leicester* (1948)
Ellis, I. C., *Records of Nineteenth Century Leicester* (1935)
Gill, Richard, *The Book of Leicester* (1985)
Hickman, Trevor, *The Melton Mowbray Album* (1997)
Hoskins W. G., *Essays in Leicestershire History* (1950)
Jenkins, Robin, *Leicestershire People* (1996)
Millward, Roy, *A History of Leicestershire and Rutland* (1985)
Morrison, John, *Hallaton, Hare-pie Scrambling and Bottle Kicking* (2000)
Nash, D. and Reeder, D., *Leicester in the Twentieth Century* (1993)
Nichols, John, *History of the Antiquities of the County of Leicester* (1791)
Paget G. and Irvine L., *Leicestershire* (1950)
Patterson, A. Temple, *Radical Leicester* (1954)
Scaysbrook, Phillip, *The Civil War in Leicestershire and Rutland* (1997)
Simmons, Jack, *Leicester Past and Present* (1974)
Squires, Anthony, *The Greys – A Long and Noble Line* (2002)
Victoria County History, Vol.IV (1958)

INDEX

References which relate to illustrations are given in **bold**.

Abbey of St Mary, Leicester, 5
Abbey Park, 5, 41, 110, **126**
advertisement from *The Uganda Argus*, **137**
Aethelfloeda, 4
Albert, Prince, 27, 40
Alexandra, Princess, 110, 111, 112, **115**
Alfred the Great, 4
All Saints church, 116
Amin, Idi, 127
Arkwright, Sir Richard, 59
Art School, New Walk, **122**
Ashby de la Zouch, **14**, 16, **97**, **99**, **108**, **109**, **110**, **115**
Attenborough, F.L., 46
Attenborough, Sir Richard, **41**, 48
Attlee, Clement, 22
Auster aircraft at Rearsby, **87-9**
aviation, 83 *et seq.*
Aylestone road, 42

Babbage, Thomas, 44
Bailey, Brian, 29
balloon ascent advertisement, **84**
Ballot Act, 109
Banks, Gordon, 43
Baptist chapel, Belvoir Street, **136**
Beacon Hill bonfire, **114**
Beaumanor, 23
Beaumont, Francis, 25
Beaumont, Sir George, 25
Beethoven, 40
Belgrave Mela, 126
bell, from Loughborough, **74-6**
Belvoir Castle, 19, 24, 27
Bennion, Charles, **18**, 23, 24
Beortfrith, 4
Billesdon, 14
Blackbrook reservoir, **65**, **66**, 73
Bleriot machine, **86**
Bosworth, battle of, 8
Bottesford church monuments, **54**
Bottle-kicking, **35**, **36**, 36, **37**
Bradgate, 8, 10, 33
Braunstone, 16, **17**, 20
brick-yard child labour, **101**
Bridgewater, Duke of, 69
Brindley, James, 69
Brookhouse, Joseph, 59, 60
Brooksby, 13
Buck, John, 46
Burton Overy, 58
Burton, John, 118
Byron, Lord, 44

canals, 69 *et seq*
Canute, King, 4
Carey, William, 124
Caribbean carnival, 126, **128**
Cartwright, Edmund, 13
Castle Donington, 16, 22, **43**
Cavendish House, 5
Cavendish Road, 54
Charles I, 13
Charnwood, 8
Charnwood Forest canal, 70, 72
Chartism, 49
Chaucer, Geoffrey, 7
Church Langton, 39
Churchill, Winston, 116
civic centre, Leicester, 119
Civil War, 17, 18, 19
Clay, Dr Patrick, **2**
Clock Tower, Leicester, **80**, 119, **129**
coin hoard, 2
Coleorton Hall, **21**, 25
Coltman, John, 59, 60, 72
Cook, James, **56**, 61, 62
Cook, Thomas, 70, **71**, **72**, 75
Cooper, Thomas, 49, 51
Corieltauvi, 2
Cossington motor car, **81**
Cottesmore hunt, **29**
Coventry, 54
Coxwell's air balloon, 83
cricket, 42
crime and punishment, 57 *et seq.*
Crow Mills, 90, **94**
Croxton Abbey, 9

D.N.A. finger-printing, 65
Danes, 4
Dare, Joseph, 42
Dawson's wheels, 61
Defoe, Daniel, 67
dinner in bell-mouth of sewer, **132**
Dishley, 73, **100**
dissolution of monasteries, 9
Diwali, 126, **127**
Domesday Book, 5
Donaldson, Canon, 122
Dudley, Guilford, 8
Dunham Massey, 23

Edward IV, 8
Edward, Prince of Wales, **32**, 34
election for Parliament, 1826, **123**, **124**

130

elephants at Melton Mowbray, **46**
Elgar, Sir Edward, 116
Elizabeth I, Queen, 7
Ellis, John, 75
Elmesthorpe, **103**
enclosure of open fields, 11
enlisting for service 1914, **45**, **46**
Enville, Staffordshire, 23
Essex Road, 54
Ethelred, 4
evacuees in Loughborough, **52**
Evesham, battle of, **6**

Fane, Lady Augusta, 30
Fenny Drayton, 14
Fernie Hunt, **31**
Ferrers, Earl, 59
Filbert Street, 43
floods in Soar valley, 90
Flower, Joan, 57
football, 43
Fosse Way, 67
fox hunting, **26**, **27**, **28**, **29**, **30**, **31**, **33**
Fox, George, 13
Foxton Locks, **77**, 82
Francis Street, 63
fulling mills, 5

Gardiner, William, 40
Garrendon Abbey, 9
Gaunt, John of, 6, 7
Geary, George, 42
Geography building of University of Leicester, 89, **91**
gibbett in Guildhall, **55**
Gill, Richard, 116
Gladstone, William, 110
Glenfield tunnel, 75
Goadby Marwood, 13
Goddard, Joseph, 118, 119
Gower, David, 42
Grace Dieu Nunnery, 9
Grace Road, 42
Great Central Railway, 77, 82
Great Glen, 58
Great Stretton, 12
Green Bicycle mystery, **58**, **59**, **60**, 64, 65
Grey Friars, 9
Grey, Jane, 8, **10**, 22
Grey, Thomas, 8, 18

Halford, Sir Richard, 19
Hall, Marshall, Q.C., 65
Hall, Robert, 124
Hallaton, 36
Hamel, Gustav, 85, **86**
Hanbury, Rev. William, 39
Handel's Messiah, 40
Hansom, Joseph, 125
Harborough, Lord, and railway, 75, 77, 78, 81
Hart, Israel, 124
Hastings, battle of, 4
Hastings, Hans Francis, 11th Earl of Huntingdon, 22
Hastings, Henry, Baron Loughborough, 22
Hastings, Theophilus, 21
Hastings, William Lord, 16
Hazelrigg, 18
Heathcoat, John, 61
Henry II, 5
Henry IV, 7
Henry VIII, 5

Heskey, Emile, 43
Highfield Street, 54
Hinckley, 15, 35, 61, 85
Horse-drawn cab at Clock Tower, **79**, **80**
hosiery, 15
Hoskins, W.G., 13, 116
Humberstone Gate, **34**, 35, 49
Huntingdon Peerage case, 21
Huntingdon, 3rd Earl, 17
Huntingdon, Selina Countess of, 20

Illingworth, Ray, 42

Jain temple, 126
Jeffries, Sir Alec, **61**, 65
Jewry Wall, 2, **3**
Jockey Club, 41
Jones, Dr Michael, 16

Kegworth air disaster, **88**
Kibworth Beauchamp, **119**
Kirby Muxloe castle, **6**, 8, 9, 16
Kirkby Mallory, **44**
Knighton Hall, 46

Labour Party, 116
lace-making, 61
Launde Abbey, 9
Lawrence, Major Pethwick, 116
laying tram lines, **78**
Lear, King, **1**
Leicester and Swannington railway, **75**
Liddle, 2
Light, Ronald, **64**
Lineker, Gary, 43
Linwood, Mary, **121**
Literary and Philosophical Society, 106
Loudon, Countess of, 21
Loughborough, *frontispiece*, **48**, **49**, **98**, **99**, **111**, **112**, 116, 118, **130**, **131**
Lovelace, Ada, 44
Lowesby Hall, 29
Lucas, Colonel, 20
Luddism, 60, 61
Lutyens War Memorial, **106**

M1 under construction, **82**
Macdonald, Ramsay, 116
machine smashing, 59, 60
Mafeking, **44**, 52
Mandela Park, 41, 104
march of unemployed men, 122, **133**, **134**
Market Bosworth, 8
Market Harborough, 19, 93, **95**, **117**
mayoral chain, 109
Medbourne, 38
Medical Officers of Health, 104
Melton Mowbray, 29
Mercia, 4
Methodism, 20
Meynell, Hugo, 26
Midland Railway under construction, 69
midnight hunt, **28**
Moira, Earl of, 22
Monmouth, Geoffrey of, 1
More, Sir Thomas, 16
Morledge Street, Leicester, fire, 94
Mount St Bernard Abbey, 124, **135**
Mowmacre Hill, 49
Mynn, Alfred, 42

Naseby, 19
National Gallery, 25
New Walk museum, 106
Nugent-Bell, Henry, 21, 22

Owston Priory, 9

Paget and Irvine, 21
Palmer, Mrs C.H., 42
peace celebrations, 1919, **51**
Pedro the Cruel, 6
Penny, Abbot William, 6
Pevsner, Nikolaus, 15
Pilcher, Percy, 83
Pilcher's Hawk glider, **84**
Pinafore, H.M.S. programme, **40**
police force established, 62
Poor Law Amendment Act, 122
pork pies, **22**, **23**, **24**
Princess Diana, **41**
Pugin, A.W.N., 124

Queniborough, 18
Quorn, 26

races at Leicester, 40
railways, 75 *et seq*
Ratae, 2, 3
Read, Robert, 41
regatta on canal, Market Harborough, **67**
Remembrance Day, Mountsorrel, **53**
Repton, 4
Richard II, 7
Richard III, 8
ridge and furrow, 4
road transport, 67 *et seq.*
Robinson, Tony, 16
Roman helmet, 2
rugby football, 43
Rupert, Prince, 18
Rutland, Earl of, 57
Rutland, John Henry, Duke of, **20**, 24, **25**, 40

sack of Leicester, 5
St Brice's Day massacre, 4
St George's church fire, 94
St Margaret's church, 116
St Margaret's pasture, 42
St Mary de Castro, 9
St Nicholas' church, 116
St Wistan, 4
Shepshed, Dolly, 83
Shepshed peace celebrations, 1919, **51**
Simpson, Mrs, **32**
Stone, Samuel, 83
See of Leicester, 116
Seventh Day Adventists, 125
Shaftesbury, Lord, 100
Shakespeare, 8, 16, 35
Shilton, Peter, 43
Shirley, Sir Robert, 14, 15
Shrewsbury, Earl of, 124
Siege of Leicester, 18, **19**
Simon de Montfort, 6, 124
Skipwith, Sir Thomas, 69
smallpox and anti-vaccination, 121

Smith, George, of Coalville, 100
Smith, 'Tanky', **57**, 62, 63
Snibston Discovery Park, 75
snow drifts at Market Harborough, **93**
Soar Navigation, 69
South Croxton church, **92**
south fields of Leicester, 40
Sporting Capital, **38**, 44
Stanford Hall, 83
Staunton Harold, **12**, 14, 15
Stephenson, Robert, 75
Stilton cheese, **25**
Stokes, Adrian, 23
Suffolk, Duchess of, 23
suffragettes, 115
Swithland reservoir, **102**
Swynford, Catherine, 6

Tebbutt's pork pies, **23**, **24**, 27
Thompson, James, 41
Three Crowns Hotel, 63, 64
Tigers and Welford Road, 43
toll gate at Loughborough, **68**
Town Hall, Leicester, 56
traffic census, 118
traffic chaos on M1, 83
Tudor, Queen Mary, 8, 9
Turner, J.M.W., 25
turnpike trusts, 67

Ulverscroft Priory, 9, 11
Unitarian Great Meeeting, 59
U.S. 82nd Airborne division at Stoughton, 86

Victoria Park tree planting, **112**
Victoria, Queen, 27, 40, 110
Villiers, George, Duke of Buckingham, 13, 14

Wallace, Kenneth 2
war effort, collecting aluminium, filling sand-bags **50**, **51**
Waterford, Marquess of, 29, 30
Waterloo, battle of, 49
Watling Street, 4
Welford Road cemetery, 106, 120
Wesley, John, 20
Wharf Street, 42
Whetstone, Joseph, 59, 60
Whipping Toms, 35
Whissendine crossing, **29**
White friars, 9
Whittle, Sir Frank, 86
Whitwick, 25
Whitwick colliery disaster, 96, 97, 98, **104**, **105**, **106**
William the Conqueror, 4, 5, 16
Williams, Brian, 73
Winstanley disappearance, 62
Winstanley, James, 20
Wistow, 16, 19
witchcraft, 57
Wolsey, 5
Wood, C.J.B., 42
Woodville, Elizabeth, 8
Wordsworth, William, 25
Wright, Bella, 64
Wycliffe, John, 6
Wyggeston hospital, 17